Afshan Malik is a writer an[...........................]y
Shaitan and the Chappal ap[.......................]*t*
(Virago 1994). She has performed her poetry in English and
Urdu, touring the UK with Manmela theatre company,
performing *We Sinful Women*, Urdu poetry from Pakistan. *Safar*
was her first stage play. She is currently writing *The Trouble
With The Human Genome Project* for which she has received an
award from The British Association and Royal Society and a
commission from Made In Wales.

Roger Williams has written plays for BBC Radio, HTV, S4C, The
Sherman Theatre, and Made In Wales.
Gulp was his first full-length stage play to be professionally
produced.
He is 23 years old and lives in Cardiff.

Lewis Davies was born in Penrhiwtyn. He is a winner of the John
Morgan Writing Prize and of an Arts Council Writing Award. He
has written two novels, *Tree of Crows* & *Work,Sex and Rugby*
and an account of a journey west on Route 66, *Freeways*.
My Piece of Happiness was his first work for the stage and was
followed by *A Travelling Man* for the *Little Country, Big War*
project, both for Made in Wales. He lives in Cardiff

PARTHIAN BOOKS

Safar

Afshan Malik

Gulp

Roger Williams

My Piece of Happiness

Lewis Davies

New Welsh Drama

PARTHIAN BOOKS

First published 1998 by Parthian Books
41 Skelmuir Road, Cardiff CF2 2PR.

Published with financial support from the
Arts Council of Wales.

ISBN 0 952 1558 77

Edited by Jeff Teare.

Printed and bound by ColourBooks, Dublin 13,
Ireland.
Typeset in New Sabon by JW.

Cover design by Griffiths & JW & Savage.

From original work by Gillian Griffiths.

Mother Tongue by Kind permission of Samia Malik
From the album Colour of the Heart 1998
Sound and Language 01502 512905

The publishers would like to thank everyone at Made
In Wales for the support in preparing this book.
Made in Wales can be contacted on
madein.wales@virgin.net

British Library Cataloguing in Publication Data.
A cataloguing record for this book is available from
the British Library.

The sharks I dodged. The tigers I slew.
What ate me up was the bed-bugs.

Bertolt Brecht

Contents

Five Shillings For A Welsh Actor

What was it Shakespeare had Hamlet say about theatre ? Mirror up to nature or something, wasn't it ? Hmm, fair enough, that's what we theatricals generally reckon it's all about, at least we do when we're not actually doing theatre; that is, the discussion of the relationship between society and drama tends to happen either in places like this (books) or in pubs after at least three pints, not in rehearsal rooms or theatres. The theory's fine but the practice ? That's down to the audience.

Some young Asian women saw *Safar* (a play about a young Asian woman) many young Cardiffians watched *Gulp* (a play about young Cardiffians) and more than a few social workers turned up for *My Piece of Happiness* (a play partly about social workers.) Is that what we mean ? Joan Littlewood used to talk (not to me, I've only met her twice and one of those times I was mainly dancing for her... but that's another theatrical anecdote luvvies) about the circular relationship to be aimed for between stage and auditorium. But surely that doesn't mean that only the incestuously inclined can relate to Oedipus, or then again, perhaps we're all incestuously inclined... Ah the search for universality...

Where was I ? Oh yes, Made In Wales and new writing theatre at the dawn of the twenty-first century. As far as I'm concerned new writing in itself has no intrinsic value (surely we've already got enough plays ?) It's only real validation lies in the degree to which it re-invents theatre for new audiences -

Discuss.

Well, if by re-invent we only mean form, then no if it's only about (or pretending to be about) the same old rubbish. Then again, old forms won't always do. It depends what audiences you're working for. The more aesthetically minded among us might well be more moved by the angle of an elbow, tone of shriek or shade of lighting than mere narrative or dramatic action but most people still tend to want (if they want anything from theatre) recognizable characters with a story to tell. It's creating new characters with something relevant to say that is the point of new writing and these three plays, in my humble opinion, all go some way to achieving this aim.

Safar was produced as one of the plays that formed a season of work at The Point, Cardiff, during the Summer of '96. (The other plays performed were *The Sea that Blazed* by Christine Watkins and *Little Sister* by Sian Evans.) I think Afshan would agree that initially I had to bully the play out of her (she certainly phoned a mutual friend to ask who this strange man was that had just invaded her office). After all, she'd never written a play before (I knew her as a short-story writer) and she had a proper job as a research scientist (at the time of writing this Afshan's writing another play for us concerning the human genome project). One thing about her being a scientist - when it came to rehearsals she was very quick to agree with what did and didn't work. Pages hit the floor, got cut, re-organized and re-written in seconds, or at least so my bitter and twisted directorial memory would have it. She was, however, quite rightly adamant about the play's poetic/non-linear (non-European ?) structure and the correct use of music (some of which was composed by her sister Samia). I suppose my favourite bit was the elephant story at the end as it enabled us to indulge in some mask and silk work. It must have more or less worked: there were frequently more than a few misty eyes at the curtain call (or perhaps that was the smoke still hanging around after the pyrotechnics). Perhaps the most successful aspect of the production was the way it brought audiences of very disparate backgrounds together - I've always been a bit of a one for socially cohesive theatre (more of the socially generative later).

Gulp was Roger Williams' first full-length play and was a big success at Chapter, Cardiff in the Summer of '97. Breaking box office records it was brought back by public demand before playing in Dublin and Newport. It was generally considered to be Cardiff's first professionally produced young, out gay play, referred to by the press as a "cultural milestone". The audience at Chapter was predominately under 35 with many first-time theatre attenders. The production was supported by Cardiff Body Positive and became something of a cult on the Cardiff gay scene and within the deaf-community (it's a long story...). Indeed, both in Cardiff and Dublin the show had an observable social effect in terms of HIV/AIDS counselling (so socially generative theatre does still exist after all). I'll long cherish the memory of the press-night reaction to Lowri Mae's Bonnie Tyler impression immediately after Keiron Self's character had just been warned that he could be HIV positive. Some of our straighter audience didn't know quite where to put themselves. Lucky it was just before the interval, bar takings were extremely healthy.

My Piece of Happiness was also premiéred at Chapter. It's subject matter of a sexual relationship between two young people with learning difficulties did not make for an easy evening in the theatre but it earned plaudits from many (though not all) involved in the issue who attended.

It was a first production for a writer new to theatre and the script had been through a long workshop process with Made In Wales prior to rehearsal. It is a well-observed piece, and was particularly well played by a fine cast. Lewis and I are still arguing about the structure and through-line of the play, in fact probably about the nature of theatre itself, but *Happiness* marked a definite arrival of a new Welsh dramatic talent. My favourite bits in this production were Dorien Thomas' timing of his response to "sex is good, isn't it George ?" and James Westaway's godlike head staring back at himself due to the miracles of modern video technology, well, when it worked...

So, three new plays by three new writers produced in Wales between 1996 and 1998. And ? Well, they are Welsh plays and they are concerned with identity but not in the usual Welsh theatrical manner. The cultural identity of *Safar* is somewhere between Pakistani and British Asian, the identity discussed in *Gulp* is sexual, and *Happiness* deals in social and existential self rather than national. Three Welsh plays in one volume not about definitions of Welshness, good grief ! And, the plays are new, all in their way first plays, dealing with world-wide issues. It has to be be fervently hoped that we don't lose these three writers given the current circumstances we are operating in.

Which brings us to the title of the essay.

In 1789 a Welsh actor-writer named Twm O'r Nant wrote

"Welsh audiences would pay five shillings to see a London actor, not one penny to see a Welsh". When I came down to run Made In Wales I turned down a previously commissioned play. The writer said if I didn't do it no-one else in Wales would. I didn't believe him. But we tried to get other people interested in *Gulp* and *Happiness* pre-production but no-one was. Oh, sure, once *Gulp* was described as 'a cultural milestone' a few people asked about it and two people thought *Safar* might do some good in schools. Yet *Gulp* played successfully for a week in Dublin and for a night in Newport while *Happiness* and *Safar* were discussed enthusiastically by companies in England and Scotland. Why ? Well, I suppose it has to do with a variety of factors: indigenous professional Welsh Theatre is only decades old, there is still no building totally committed to a new writing policy in Wales, Cardiff's fringe theatre has been dominated by a physical theatre aesthetic since the early '70's (unlike, for example, London, Dublin or Edinburgh, by a text-based one) and that there's relatively little going on (it's a small country) so that most of the actors and many of the writers end up in London anyway. (Some things don't change then, Twm...). Yet these writers are, pound for pound, as good as many I've come across in London (or New York and Chicago for that matter) who have received much more attention.

Still, the audiences that saw them enjoyed their nights in the theatre, or at least most of them did, give or take the odd critic (sometimes very odd) and disgruntled pro. The writers have all gone on to write other things and Made in Wales survives (just) to fight another day. Let me tell you about our next little epic, Cardiff's first professional Black and Asian play that we're taking to London, *Giant Steps* by Othniel Smith and then there's Larry Allan's techno-musical about New Labour and the death of Socialism. Well, hopefully this list will continue into the twenty-first century. Meanwhile - enjoy !

OM MANI PADME HUM

Jeff Teare
July 1998

In rehearsal.

Safar
[JOURNEY]

A PLAY BY AFSHAN MALIK

Safar was premiéred by Made In Wales at The Point, Cardiff in September 1996 with the following cast:

Ismaat	Brigitta Roy
Jamil, her father	Shiv Grewal
Zeenat, her mother	Shireen Shah
Rhiannon, Linda,	
Headmistress &	
Little Elephant	Karin Diamond
Jinh, Gary,	
Maulvi & Big Elephant	James Westaway

Directed by Jeff Teare
Designed by Sue Mayes
Lighting by Dennis Charies
Assistant Director Rebecca Gould
Assistant Designer Kate Lynham

Music - "Classical North Indian". Ismaat is sitting in the centre of the stage. Video of Asian immigrant families arriving in Britain (Stanstead Airport etc.) in the 60's and 70's.

Voices Over -
Immigrant/ identity/ exile/ Welsh/ traveller/ Pakistani/ mussafar/ English/ identity/ angrezi/ gora/ kala/ confusion/ shame/ sharam/ haya/ izzat/ belonging/ where are you from?/ kahan say Aaee ho?/ O ble 'dych chi'n dod ?

Silence. Darkness except for the light over Ismaat at the centre of the stage, who has not yet moved. She raises her head.

ISMAAT   I am two people.

Both of me exist, in my body, but which one is real.

I look at other people and wonder if they too have another person inside them.

I have a short memory because there are no holes for my past to fit into.

It is unexpected, unreal, except that it happened.

One of me knows it happened. I can remember fragments of things, with large gaps in between. I remember feelings for which I have no words.

The other me does not remember much. I am like a sponge. I soak up experiences from around me. I make their memories mine. I magically recall the same things, and laugh at the right places, and nod knowingly. It makes the gaps smaller on the outside, but inside the gap grows until it has turned and twisted my insides.

Those voices keep calling me.

They keep calling me back, calling me back...

Music - "North Indian classical scale". A woman's voice singing "The Calling Song" music by Samia Malik, words by Afshan Malik.

ISMAAT   Calling me back...

Rhiannon enters.

ISMAAT   Time, Waqt.

RHIANNON   Time, Amser.

ISMAAT   Time, Waqt.

RHIANNON   Time, Amser.

ISMAAT   Time Waqt.

Ismaat sees Rhiannon.

ISMAAT   Do I know you ? What are we doing here ?

RHIANNON   Well, there I was, into the third stage of my meditation, focused on my seventh Chakra, connecting with the universe, and I had a sudden call. I didn't even get time to prepare. Wham bam and here I am.

ISMAAT   You got a call?

RHIANNON   Yes, strongest calling I ever had.

ISMAAT   You mean it was me ? I called you ?

RHIANNON   Yes.

ISMAAT   Who are you?

RHIANNON   I am Rhiannon. Normally I work as a librarian. The Spiritual and Magical being my field...especially Welsh legends. But in my own time I am preparing to be a spiritual guide.

ISMAAT   Oh no, does that mean, I died ?

RHIANNON   No, you're not dead. You are in a trance. Prepare yourself my girl. We are off on the trip of a life-time.

ISMAAT   How do you know ?

RHIANNON   I pick-up everything from your aura. You know all this yourself.

ISMAAT   Where are you taking me ?

RHIANNON   It is not I taking you. It is you, taking me. This journey is yours.

ISMAAT   Journey?

RHIANNON   Into the past...

ISMAAT   I don't feel very well...

RHIANNON   Let's sit here, in the shade of this tree.

A tree appears. The two women sit down. A champagne bottle flies into view.

ISMAAT   Hey, look at this. A bottle of champagne. Moet et Chandon, 1947. This has been here a long time. Nearly 50 years.

RHIANNON   Don't rub!

But Ismaat has already started to rub the bottle. Suddenly there is a flash and The Jinh, appears on a trapeze.

JINH   Thank you for calling me oh mistress (*he kneels on one knee*). Your wish is my command. (*He takes her hand and kisses it.*)

ISMAAT   OK, you guys. Enough is enough. Now, stop messing around. Here I am, with a woman who says I called her through the ether to be my spiritual guide, and a man who seems to have been in a champagne bottle for 50 years. This isn't funny. I am beginning to get distressed.

JINH   Sweet mistress. Don't distress yourself. In the last 3,000 years I've never had the extreme pleasure to serve one as beautiful as you. 50 years in a champagne bottle and then to come out and see you. What a sight for these eyes.

RHIANNON   We don't need you, Genie, or whoever you are. We're perfectly OK on our own.

JINH   I hear there is a great journey, safar, into the past. You and I both (*points to Rhiannon*), guiding Ismaat, making it possible.

RHIANNON   You and me ? I thought Genies are supposed to live in oil lamps, not bottles.

JINH   Jinh, please! Genie is a Westernised mispronunciation and a thorough misrepresentation of my elite and humble people. The bottle is a sign of the times. Things change. Nothing can remain the same, not even the sun.

RHIANNON   I knew it was something big, the way I was summoned by Ismaat. I've never had a stronger calling... Well, let's do it then!

Music - They dance in a circle. Black Out.
Lights up.

RHIANNON   So, Jinh, is it true you can grant us anything ?

JINH   Only if my mistress commands.

RHIANNON   Well, Ismaat, since you called me here so unexpectedly and I wasn't at all prepared, what say you organise a feast ?

ISMAAT   What do you want?

RHIANNON   Hot doughnuts with chocolate sauce to start!

ISMAAT   Jinh, get some hot doughnuts in chocolate sauce.

JINH   It's been sometime since I used my magic. Nearly 50 years. The words change with each time. I need to meditate.

JINH   Yeh-ham-kahan-aagaye-hain

Nothing happens.

JINH   Aaj-ya-kal-kayamat-aanay-wali-hai

Nothing happens.

Ismaat and Rhiannon look at each other and then at their watches. Jinh concentrates for a few moments.

JINH   I've got it, wait. Ji-hazoor-ham-kalay-aadmi-hain.

There is a flash and a plate of doughnuts appears. The two women exclaim delight. The three of them sit and start to eat.

ISMAAT   You know, when I was a little girl, I used to pretend to be a great singer. I used to stand in front of the mirror with a pretend microphone and sing Indian film songs. Until one day... One day, I was standing in front of the mirror in my fantasy world   and I looked out. We used to live in a street of terraced houses and across the road I could see this girl standing in front of her mirror, doing the same thing. Standing there, with a pretend mike, pretend singing. There were all these rows and rows of houses all around me, all full of people, girls, like me, pretending, pretending. *(Sighs)* But, I wasn't like them really.

RHIANNON   Why was that ?

ISMAAT   They were all white.

RHIANNON   So?

ISMAAT   I was different. Even when I try to fit in people keep seeing me as different. Complete strangers, meet me at a party, first thing they say, where are you from ?

JINH   What do you say?

ISMAAT   Splott *(note - an area of Cardiff)*. But they don't believe me. They don't want to know where I'm from. They want to know WHERE I'm from. My genetic history. Where were my parents born ? Where were my grand parents born ? What the hell am I doing in Splott they think. When I came to this country I couldn't speak a word of English. That made me feel different...

RHIANNON   Yeh, and my first language is Welsh... I was about five before I realised that everybody didn't speak it.

ISMAAT   I ended up speaking a mish-mash of the two... We used to call it Gulabi Urdu, pink Urdu.

RHIANNON   I still get my friends laughing when I'm on the phone to my Mum and I'm talking in Welsh and they get the occasional English word like "camcorder".

ISMAAT   Or "euro-tunnel"

RHIANNON   "Internet"...

ISMAAT   "Sex"...

RHIANNON   Sex is Rhyw in Welsh.

ISMAAT AND JINH   Rhyw...

RHIANNON   No, rrriiww...

ISMAAT   Do you know, there are more than 50 different words for love in Urdu.. I only know a few of them...

RHIANNON   Go on then...

ISMAAT   My Urdu's so rusty...Ishq, Muhabbat, Pyar...

JINH   Ulfat...

ISMAAT   What? Oh yes, ulfat... What about "love" in Welsh?

RHIANNON   Cariad. What about sex in urdu?

ISMAAT   You know, I don't know. The only rude words I know

are the ones the white kids used to shout at the Asian kids. I still don't know what they meant.

JINH   Jans. Sex is Jans...

ISMAAT   I never knew that.

JINH   It means gender...

ISMAAT   English - Angrezi...

RHIANNON   Angrezi... English - Sais

ISMAAT   White - Gora...

RHIANNON   White? er... *(Whispers)* Twll din pob Sais *(note - loosely translated as "Bugger off English git")*

JINH   It's time to start the journey. Ismaat, tell me what is in your heart ?

ISMAAT   In my heart?

JINH   The question ? The meaning you've been looking for ?

ISMAAT   I don't know!

JINH   I think you do...
The Jinh gestures to Rhiannon. Rhiannon sits Ismaat in front of her.

RHIANNON Close your eyes Ismaat. Close your eyes and breathe slowly. In, out, in, out. Let yourself feel relaxed. Let go and let whatever comes come into your mind.

ISMAAT I don't know who I am. Yes. That's it. Always the same feeling. Who am I ? Who am I ? Rhiannon knows she is Welsh. She is surrounded by her own history, her own sense of identity, her family. You know you are a Jinh. But I don't know who I am. I know it sounds crazy. But I don't know who I am. Not in here. Not in my heart.

JINH So you don't think of yourself as Welsh?

ISMAAT No.

JINH Pakistani ?

ISMAAT No.

JINH English ?

ISMAAT No !

JINH British ?

ISMAAT Oh god, I don't know !

RHIANNON What's the confusion about Ismaat?

ISMAAT It's a long story.

RHIANNON   It's OK, we are in a timeless place. You can take as long as you want.

ISMAAT   It's not just the confusion about the language, who I am, where I'm from. It's not just that. It's everything. Everything. Maybe it was my fault. Maybe that's why they died.

RHIANNON   Who?

ISMAAT   My mum and dad. They were both under 50. They were so young. I never expected it to happen. I couldn't believe it. I can't believe it even now. Everything is so confused. When I stop to think about how I feel my head starts to spin and I'm afraid, I'm afraid.

RHIANNON   What are you afraid of Ismaat ?

ISMAAT   I'm afraid that it's all true.

Music - "Maan-ki-zabaan" song by Samia Malik.

ISMAAT   When I first went off to University. I used to call home every week, sometimes nearly every day, especially at the beginning. It was expected you know? Since I was an only child. It was quite a pressure. But living away from home was brilliant. I was free to do whatever I wanted. I shared a house with Linda who was an artist, and Gary, who was doing psychology.

Ismaat joins "Linda" and "Gary". They sit around a fireplace passing a joint.

LINDA   Nietszche killed God...

ISMAAT   Who the hell's Nietszche?

GARY   I still don't understand why you won't cook me chicken curry and parathas Ismaat?

ISMAAT   Piss off Gary. There's more to me than curries.

The telephone rings in the background.

ISMAAT   Well go on then!

GARY   I answered it yesterday.

Gary goes out to answer the phone. The two women start to eat chocolate and laugh. We can hear Gary in the background.

GARY   Yes she lives here. This is her flatmate. Yes. Gary Johnson. Yes she is here shall I call her? Oh I see.

The two women stop what they are doing and start listening.

GARY   Oh my God. When? Oh no. Yes yes. What shall I do ? We could do that. Yes. OK then. OK.

He comes into the room looking very shaken.

ISMAAT   Who was that?

GARY   The police.

ISMAAT   What is it? What's happened?

Gary comes and sits near her. He holds her hands.

GARY   Ismaat.

ISMAAT   Gary, you're scaring me. Stop messing. Is this a joke?

GARY   Ismaat, I'm so sorry Ismaat. Your parents, they had an accident in their car.

ISMAAT   Ammi, Abbu!

The light darkens. "Linda" and "Gary" exit.

ISMAAT   Mum and Dad. Killed outright. I never got to tell them how I felt. I used to have these dreams. Still do, like a film in which it's up to me to save them. If only I could get there, on time, usually just a matter of minutes. I'm standing in the phone box and I have no change and if I can't make the call they are going to die and I just can't get it together. I just can't. I sat laughing, smoking, eating, while they were dying. Why didn't I feel anything? Sometimes, in other dreams, they would sit there, with me, round a table and we'd all laugh about the time I thought they'd died. I was left with nothing to hold on to. Floating free. Not knowing which way to turn. But what I really want to know is why? Why did my parents leave their home country? Why did they come here to die? Why did they come here and die and leave me alone, not knowing who I am?

JINH   You can go back.

RHIANNON   You can't change anything...

JINH   But you can go back and understand... Ji-hazzoor-ham-kalay-aadmi-hain.

There is a flash and the scene changes. Jamil is sitting in the centre on a prayer mat. He is about 27 (younger than in the rest of play). Ismaat looks at Jamil.

ISMAAT   That's my father. He is so young. How can he be here. He is dead. This is my grandparents' house. I remember it. Oh look, the grape vine is so small. When I used to come here it used to cover the whole wall. I used to try and swing on it and I thought there was a Jinh that lived here... I don't understand...

RHIANNON   Time, Amser

ISMAAT   Time Waqt.

JINH   Amser, Waqt, illusions of the mind.

Ismaat goes to touch her father, he stops her with a gesture.

JAMIL   Ismaat , beti, how nice to see you.

ISMAAT   Abbu, you can see me. Oh Abbu.

JAMIL   Sit down. I am glad you have come.

ISMAAT   You were expecting me?

JAMIL   I had a dream. *(laughs)* I was in the mosque, for 30 days and 30 nights. I was reciting the Quran. Reading. Praying. Thinking. You see I have to make a choice. A choice about the path for my future life.

ISMAAT   What's the choice you have to make?

JAMIL   The choice is to go and follow my path. I am preparing for my journey, to the West. I will leave soon. There is no work here any more. Since the British left, it has been dire.

ISMAAT   Have you thought about this properly? Do you know what it means? You know who you are. It is such a precious gift, identity.

JAMIL   It is a precious gift yes. I know. There is no work here any more. I have to travel to find work, employment. If it is written in my kismet, then it has to be so.

ISMAAT   No Dad, you can change it. You can choose your own path.

JAMIL   There is nothing here for me. Poverty, struggles, confusion.

ISMAAT   But what will you find in The West?

JAMIL   A place where things are better. Pakistan is too corrupt. The politicians cover-up scandals with money. I cannot live in a state like this and I don't want my children to grow up in a state like this. In Britain, every thing will be organised. No corruption. A proper system of democracy. A good socialist system. Education for all, poor or rich, health service for all, poor or rich.

ISMAAT   Your ideas about what Britain is like are a dream Abbu. It is not like that. It is not a place where the people count, no more than Pakistan. The democracy is a sham.

JAMIL   Don't you see. I have to do this. The British have gone from here. The country has been bled dry.

ISMAAT   Listen to me Dad, Abbu. Listen to me. You can't go Dad. Don't go. This is where we belong. Dad, it's dangerous Dad. Don't go. You and Ammi, you die out there. Listen to me. You died and you left me alone. Don't go !

Jamil exits.

ISMAAT   Why can't he hear me ? Why won't he change his mind ?

RHIANNON   What is done is done. All you can do is learn from it.

ISMAAT   My father is brainwashed. What am I saying ? My father is dead. But just now, I saw him like he was before I was born. And he was brainwashed. Brought up in the British Raj, he was in awe of the British, he thought they were civilised. He thought they had answers. His whole generation were like that. Passive.

JINH   Maybe you don't understand the choices he had.

RHIANNON   So your parents moved, with you as a child, to The West.

ISMAAT   Yes, we moved a lot and settled in Cardiff. In those days, there were only two streets with immigrants in. There were just a few of us. Few enough to be a novelty

RHIANNON   What about your mother ? Didn't she mind losing her home ?

ISMAAT   My mother? I never felt like I knew anything about her. She kept herself so hidden.

JINH   It is time for us to visit your mother.

Music - "Maan-Ki-Zabaan". Lights down. Zeenat is asleep.

ISMAAT   Oh my god. Ammi. She looks so young. I wonder when this is?

JINH   1967.

Video of Pakistan/India at the time of partition, people travelling in droves. Children crying. Photographs of fire, looting, headlines. Jinh, Rhiannon and Ismaat watch.

RHIANNON   What is this?

JINH   1947. The partition between India and Pakistan.The British have left. Hindustan has been divided into two countries. India and Pakistan. Thousands of families had to leave their ancestral homes. People who had lived together in harmony for years, Muslims, Sikhs, Hindus. Suddenly they all became divided. There was rioting and looting.

RHIANNON   Sounds frightening.

JINH   Fear beyond belief.

ISMAAT   1947, nearly 50 years ago.

JINH   And right now, it is still your mothers' youth. She is only 20 years away from the partition.

RHIANNON   Sshh. look.

Zeenat gets up as if she is sleep walking. She speaks to the audience.

ZEENAT   When I was a child, I watched my mother die. I was
four.
We were leaving India. Muhajars. Because of the partition.
She was trying to save me, hide me from the looters. So, it was

my fault. My fault.

We left India because we were Muslim
We left Pakistan because we were poor.
Now I am here and my heart is broken.

When I wake up, screaming, in the night.
My husband tells me to be quiet.
"Quiet!" he says. "What will our white neighbours think of us
Pakistanis if I scream ?"
So, I swallow my screams until they turn inwards and twist my
insides.

I don't have the words.
Here, in this cold and distant land.
I don't have the language.
That place is gone.
But it is still here, in my head, in my heart.

ISMAAT   Mum, Ammi...

She reaches out her hand. Zeenat does not see her. She turns away and is led away by Jinh.

ISMAAT   When we came to the UK, I was 11. We flew here, from Karachi to Heathrow. So we couldn't bring much stuff. I took virtually nothing with me. Not even my books, or dolls. It was like losing my childhood in one clean sweep.

Jinh and Rhiannon enter with the dolls and old school books.

ISMAAT   My dolls. Here are my dolls. Look, this one, she's called Reshmaan, because she's got hair like reshum, silk. Here - feel. And this one is Heer because she looks like a tragic heroine. Just look at her big sad eyes. And if you put water here it leaks out of her eyes and she looks like she is crying. And this one, she's called Moti because she's so skinny. Oh look. Here's a school book. It's got the national anthem. Oh, it looks faded. I remember dropping this book in the pond. But, I can just make out the words.
Pak sar zameen shad bad
Qou-a-tay yaqeen shad bad
something something alishan
something something zamin shad bad.
We used to sing this every day in the school assembly. Oh, here is Bunder, my favourite monkey. He is engaged to Heer. Shall we get them married. I know, I could let them kiss.

She holds them both up and tries to get them to kiss. But then she lowers them, lowers her own head, and looks upset.

ISMAAT   It's no good. It's too late now.

JINH   Ji hazoor nam-kalay-aadmi-hain!
There is a flash and a cooker appears. Zeenat enters and starts cooking with it. Jamil follows her into the room.

ZEENAT   Oh there you are Jamil. I couldn't light the paraffin heater it was freezing all day. The milkman called and I had no money, I didn't know what to say. I hate this angrezi stuff.

JAMIL   English.

ZEENAT   English sminglish. Who cares ? It's all farangi language. Where is the poetry in it. Nowhere. Listen. The aata is running out. You'll have to pop over to Afzal Bhai's shop to get me some more. And some tomatoes. No not straight away. We'll eat first. That reminds me. Begum *(Emphasises this word)* Afzal called. Masha Allah, that woman has really taken on some colours. Yesterday she lived in a dusty veranda, and today she is Begum Afzal. Came to show me her new gold jewellry. Who does she think she is ? Just because her husband runs a stupid grocery store. Here pass me those onions. *(Jamil passes the onion and dips his fingers in a pot and starts to eat).* No keep your fingers out of the salan. We're having Sarson ka saag, paneer and stuffed parathas today. Get the yogurt out would you and put it in the bowl. Have you lit the paraffin heater yet ? Oh yes, and you've got to tell that daughter of yours. She spends all her time lost in a day dream. Ismaat *(Shouts)*? I've been calling her for the last hour. And she's sitting there gazing into space. Pagli, that's what they'd call her back home.

JAMIL   And I'm pagla. Your pagla.

ZEENAT   Hut paray...What's gotten into you ?

JAMIL   I'm just deliriously happy to see my gorgeous wife.

ZEENAT   Ssh, what will Ismaat think if she hears you ?

JAMIL   She'll think I'm pagla. Pagal pagal. Ham tumharay

pagal. *(He tries to dance with her).*

ZEENAT   Oh look the parathas are burning. Ismaat. Get down here. Come on Jamil. Quit fooling, let's get the table ready.

JAMIL   I don't need food. Just let me gaze into your eyes *(he starts to sing)* "Khilona. Jaan kar tum to mera dil tor jatay ho." *(This is a famous old Indian film song).*

ZEENAT   What's happened ? Come on. I know the signs.

JAMIL   I don't know what you mean.

ZEENAT   What have you done ? All this sweet talk ? What's it about ?

JAMIL   Ismaat. Beti. Come down here.

Ismaat is standing transfixed with Rhiannon and Jinh all this time. She looks at them.

JINH   You can talk to your parents if you want to.

RHIANNON   All you have to do is walk into the room.

ISMAAT   Just walk in ?

Ismaat starts to walk to the centre of the stage.

ISMAAT   Ammi, Abbu...

ZEENAT   There you are. I've been calling you for the last hour.

Ismaat rushes over and puts her arms around Zeenat.

ISMAAT   Oh Ammi, Ammi. *(She starts to cry).*

ZEENAT   Array, what's the matter ?

JAMIL   What is it Ismaat ?

ISMAAT   It was like a bad dream. Like you'd both gone away and left me, all on my own.

ZEENAT   We have gone away. All three of us. Gone away from home. But at least we're together.

She also starts to cry. Jamil puts his arms around both of them.

JAMIL   What's this? My two most favourite women in the world. Both crying because I've come home? Now I really feel like a pagla.

Zeenat laughs. He tickles both of them.

ZEENAT   Now come on. Stop this masti. Hai. The parathas have cooled off.
Jamil lays a cloth on the floor.

JAMIL   Mem Sahib. Please be seated *(He gestures).* And choti mem sahib too. Let this servant bring you his offerings. Please please. *(He ushers them both down).*

He brings plates of food from the cooker and they start to eat.

JAMIL   What's this ? Not eating much Ismaat ? It's your favourite meal today.

ISMAAT   I'm not hungry.

ZEENAT   What are you talking about ? Did you eat at school ?

ISMAAT   No, no, I....

She looks around to where Jinh and Rhiannon are.

JAMIL   So, how was school ?

ISMAAT   Terrible. You said Britain had the best education system in the world, didn't you Abbu ? You said that people from all over the world come here to study.

ZEENAT   One of your fathers' exaggerations.

ISMAAT   I don't feel hungry. I think I'll watch TV.

She goes back to join Jinh and Rhiannon.

ZEENAT   Now Jamil, are you going to tell me ?

JAMIL   You know Zeenat, all the things I do are for us, I always do the best for us that I can.

ZEENAT   The best in whose opinion? Not mine that's for sure.

JAMIL   I came here because I thought it was best for all of us.

ZEENAT   You came here because Pakistan was too corrupt for a puritan like you. You didn't give a thought to me or my happiness.

JAMIL   Zeenat. It hurts me to hear you talk like that. Look at all the things we have here. It is brilliant.

ZEENAT   Don't give me all this brainwashing. Just tell me, tell me what you've done now.

JAMIL   I've found us a house. It's in Cardiff, a place called Riverside. Don't you think that is romantic. *(Note - one of Cardiff's most multi-cultural areas.)*

ZEENAT   I am sick of moving. Every two days we pack up and move. What is it? What are we running from? You've ruined my life. I can't bear it, I can't bear it. You and your daughter, you've cursed my life.

JAMIL   Please don't shout, Ismaat will hear you.

ZEENAT   I curse the day I laid my eyes on you. Hai Allah, Hai Allah, where shall I go, how shall I get out of this hell?

JAMIL   Alright then. Have it your own way. All day I work. I do my best and what do I get?

ZEENAT   You think you can shout at me, just because I'm on my own, you think you can boss me about ?

ISMAAT   Ammi, Abbu, please, please!

Lights dim to three tight areas on Ismaat, Zeenat and Jamil standing separately. They talk directly to the audience, overlapping the beginnings and ends of speeches.

ISMAAT   I don't know how to talk to my parents. When they brought me here, I lost my language. I lost my culture. I lost my grandparents, aunts, uncles, friends. I had no-one around me who I could talk to. I had no love at home because my parents were too busy coping.

ZEENAT   I couldn't cope. I hated my life. I had nightmares. I hated my daughter Ismaat. I hated my husband Jamil. I felt so isolated. I could not speak the language. I lost my friends, my family. I lost myself. I had no life. It was worse than dying.

JAMIL   I couldn't cope. They wouldn't recognise my qualifications. I had to work in the iron mills. I felt shattered. I felt isolated. I felt so small. I felt guilty.

All three speak together -

I felt so isolated. You never listened to how I felt.

ZEENAT   All day long. Lighting the paraffin heater. The smells in the house. Condensation on the windows. Damp disgusting smells. It was not my choice, not my life.

JAMIL   All day long. Coping with hostility. No friends. No-one on my side. And when I came home, more problems, more rows, more and more guilt. I had burn marks on my feet, where the hot metal had spattered me. Why did I leave home ?

ZEENAT   Why did you make us leave ?

ISMAAT   At school, they made me wear a skirt, but according to Muslim law, I couldn't bare my legs.

She puts on a school skirt.

JAMIL   It is against our custom for our women to wear skirts. It is forbidden. I will not allow it.

ISMAAT   But Abbu, I wore skirts in my last school in Pakistan.

JAMIL   Chup Karo, that was different. You were nine then, now you are eleven.

ISMAAT   So, I had to wear both. Salwar and skirt. One to keep my father happy. One to keep my headmistress happy.

Ismaat puts on a salwar underneath her skirt.

ISMAAT   All the kids laughed at me. They laughed so much. I looked ridiculous. I was so ashamed I wanted to die.

ZEENAT   All day long I would spend in the damp smelly house. There was no light around me. There was no light in my heart.

JAMIL   All day long I would spend in the mills. It was dark when I left the house. Dark when I came home. There was no light around me. There was no light in my heart.

ISMAAT   Ammi, Abbu, listen to me. You never listened to me. I don't know who I am. Life is hard without roots.

ZEENAT   All day long I would dream. In my dream I was in Pakistan. I was there in my garden. Then she would come home and shatter my dreams. Always there. Asking for things. I hated her. She was my daughter but I hated her.

ISMAAT   I never felt like you loved me Ammi. You never hugged me or touched me. I felt so alone.

Ismaat moves towards her mother but the mother turns away, leaving Ismaat's arms outstretched.

ZEENAT   Where is it written that a woman has no choices in life? Where were my dreams now ? In Pakistan I was proud of who I was. My family had Izzat, respect. In Britain I am a wog. An immigrant. An illiterate stupid woman. This is not my life.

Music - "We'll Keep A Welcome In The Hillside"

JAMIL   *(Reading a letter)* Dear mother, we are settling down well and happy. This is a wonderful country. The roads are so clean.

Public transport is wonderful. Zeenat loves her new house. You know how house-proud she always is. She is busily setting out everything. Ismaat is really enjoying her new school. People here are very friendly and welcoming. Everything is clean and ordered. We are so happy we came, though we miss you all very much.

Sound of breaking glass and shouting voices.

VOICES   Go home Pakis, go home.

Black Out. Lights up. Ismaat is reading a teenage girl's magazine. Zeenat enters to her carrying a hammer.

ISMAAT   Ammi ! What on earth are you doing ?

ZEENAT   I'm going to nail the curtains to the wall. Now that I've made them I just want to get them up, much better than tracks. Anyway, it's never light for long...

ISMAAT   Why do you have to sew everything ? Why can't you buy ready made curtains like normal parents ? It's embarrassing. Rebecca's mum wouldn't dream of sewing anything. Sewing is so common.

ZEENAT   We can't buy ready made curtains, we don't have the money.

ISMAAT   Well, at least her Mum doesn't wear stupid clothes.

ZEENAT   Salwar kameez is our national dress.

ISMAAT   I hate Salwars they look so stupid. They're disgusting.

ZEENAT   It doesn't matter what you think. You're going to have a new suit for Eid. What colour do you want ? Look, this one is french chiffon. What a lovely blue.

ISMAAT   Oh Ammi, do I have to ?

ZEENAT   Come on beti, it's Eid.

ISMAAT   But I hate these things, shiny bright. They draw attention. I want black. I want black so no one will notice what I am wearing. So no-one will see me. Mum, why don't you wear jeans ? They're so comfy.

ZEENAT   Salwars are very comfy too.

ISMAAT   They're so common. Why do we have to dress like Pakis ?

Lights. Ismaat and Zeenat are being interviewed by headmistress.

HEADMISTRESS   These immigrant parents are such a problem. They don't understand about their children's' education. They are a drain on our system. In my school there are 30% blacks. 30%! And I'm expected to cater for their needs. They demand days off for their festivals, they want special diets and the girls wear trousers! This isn't what I trained for, this isn't what my father fought the war for.

Ismaat and Zeenat enter and sit in front of the headmistress.

HEADMISTRESS   Well, Mrs Awan, it's nice to meet you at last.

Zeenat nods. Ismaat squirms.

HEADMISTRESS   Ismaat is doing very well in her studies. But she is a very quiet girl.

ZEENAT   What did she say?

ISMAAT   She says I'm doing OK.

HEADMISTRESS   What did she say?

ISMAAT   She asked what you said.

ZEENAT   Tell her that's good.

ISMAAT   She says that's good.

HEADMISTRESS   Good, Good...

ZEENAT   What did she say?

ISMAAT   She said "Good, Good !"

HEADMISTRESS   I feel, however, that she should play a bigger part in school life.

ZEENAT   What did she say?

ISMAAT   She said I should mix more.

ZEENAT   No, no...

HEADMISTRESS   Anyway, so nice to meet you Mrs Awan.

ZEENAT   What did she say?

ISMAAT   She said what a waste of time it was meeting you!

ZEENAT   Tell her she's a rude pig. Bloody Goras, who the hell do they think they are ?

Zeenat exits. The Headmistress exits, after confiscating Ismaat's magazine.

ISMAAT   If only every one hadn't made friends before I got here. I might have stood a chance. But I know the truth really. Even if they hadn't made them they wouldn't want to play with me. I've got greasy hair. And I'm curry smell.
I watched Elizabeth today. She's got long straight hair, it's brown. Brown's so lovely not boring and black like mine. She was sitting surrounded by other girls. They were all laughing. Then they looked at me. "Curry smell is a nose bag," someone said. I'm so ashamed I wash really hard in the bath but I can't get the colour out. I don't feel like curry smell. But I must be.
Yesterday I asked Abbu what a wog is. Wog wog, they shout at school whichever way I go. At first I thought it was like hello. So

I said it back to them. But they all laughed so much that I was embarrassed. Abbu looked embarrassed so I thought it must be rude word like 'fuck' so I looked it up in the dictionary.

Western Oriental Gentleman. Did they think I'm a man? I even have to speak for Ammi. At school, or at the doctors, or at the shop. She makes me say things. She won't talk herself. I have to do it. She says she can't, but I don't believe her.

I've been thinking about it for hours now, and I think I've worked out why. She is using me as a servant because all the other servants have been left behind in Pakistan. But why me? Doesn't she love me.? It certainly feels like she doesn't. I think and think, and suddenly I realise the truth in a flash. Why else would she use me, make me do all the talking to the goras? She is probably not my real mum. Yes, that must be it. It's all making sense now. My real Mum must be sophisticated and cool and together and I bet she can talk to anyone. I wonder where she is?

Zeenat enters.

ISMAAT   It's not going to work anymore.

ZEENAT   What?

ISMAAT   I know the truth.

ZEENAT   What are you talking about ?

ISMAAT   I know you're not my real Mum, you may as well admit it Ammi.

ZEENAT   Don't be stupid, go to your room!

ISMAAT   No!

ZEENAT   Go, now. *(She shouts)*

ISMAAT   I know you're my step-mum and you're using me as a slave, well I won't do it anymore I won't, I won't, I won't.

ZEENAT   Upstairs! *(She shouts.)* Get to your room.

ISMAAT   I hate you step mother !

Zeenat slaps Ismaat. Ismaat rushes to "her room".

ISMAAT   They kept it secret all these years but I can sense the truth. I can hear Ammi sobbing downtairs and my father murmuring. She's filling him with lies, I hate her !

Jamil walks in looks at Ismaat. Ismaat looks frightened.

JAMIL   Come downstairs and say sorry to your Ammi !
Now !
(Offering a bar of chocolate and winking.) Now...

Ismaat smiles and takes the chocolate before running downstairs. Lights. Ismaat and Jamil are playing chess.

JAMIL   No no, if you bring the queen out now, I'll be able to take it, with my knight, see.

ISMAAT   Oh yes. I'll think again.

ISMAAT   Abbu...

JAMIL   Yes...

ISMAAT   Can I call you Dad?

JAMIL   What's wrong with Abbu?

ISMAAT   Nothing. I just want to call you Dad.

JAMIL   I feel strange, you calling me Dad.

ISMAAT   I feel strange calling you Abbu.

JAMIL   (*Jamil laughs*).How about a compromise, sometimes you call me Dad, sometimes Abbu ?

ISMAAT   OK Dad. (*As she is saying this, Zeenat enters.*)

ZEENAT   What is this Dad schmaz ? Speak to your father with some respect.

ISMAAT   I did.

ZEENAT   Hmmpf.

ISMAAT   Ammi. ?

ZEENAT   Yes ?

ISMAAT   Can I call you Mum, just sometimes ?

ZEENAT   Mum ? Dad ? You think we are angrezi huh ?

ISMAAT   There's nothing wrong with it.

Jamil and Zeenat look at each other.

ZEENAT   Well, I suppose not. Now, how long are you two going to carry on playing chess ?

JAMIL   There, check mate.

ISMAAT   Oh Dad, you always beat me.

JAMIL   Well, it's getting late and you have school tomorrow.

ISMAAT   Dad, Abbu, tell me more of the elephant story ?

ZEENAT   Elephant story. Good god girl, you are fifteen now. It is not fitting for a girl your age to want bedtime stories.

ISMAAT   But he never finished it. The two elephants have lost their parents and their homes and they are wandering about searching, I don't know what for. And I go to sleep and I dream about them and I want to know what happened.

JAMIL   The hathi and his sathi. I promise to tell you more of the story, but not tonight. And one of these days, you never know, we might even get to the end.

ISMAAT   Oh. All right then. Good night.

ALL THREE   Shab bakhair.

ISMAAT   Ankhen band.

ZEENAT   Naak band.

JAMIL   Kaan band.

Lights down. Music - "Maan Ki Zabaan" until "God Save The Queen, A Fascist Regime" by The Sex Pistols crashes in. Ismaat is dancing with Gary , both dressed as punks. Zeenat and Jamil enter. Jamil walks over to the radiogram ("played" by Rhiannon) and turns off the sound.

ISMAAT   Mum, Dad, this is Gary, a friend from school.

Jamil steps forward and Gary takes a step back. Jamil holds out his hand.

JAMIL   How do you do Gary ?

GARY   Er, hello...

JAMIL   You are at Ismaat's school then ?

GARY   Yeah.

JAMIL   That song, I recognise the words, very patriotic, no ?

GARY   Um no. Not patriotic. The opposite actually Mr Awan.

JAMIL   I've always admired the Queen. She is a great ruler.

ISMAAT   Oh god.

GARY   My mum's a great supporter of the Royal family. She collects all the mugs.

JAMIL   Mugs ?

GARY   You know, like from the Coronation ? She keeps them wrapped up because she thinks one day they will be worth a lot of money.

JAMIL   So, you are very patriotic ?

GARY   No sir, I believe in anarchy.

JAMIL   I see.

GARY   Well um, time I was on my way. Nice to meet to Mr um Mrs um Awan. Bye Ismaat.

Gary exits.

JAMIL   That's one thing about this country, every day I learn something new.

ZEENAT: Hai Allah ! What on earth have you done to your beautiful hair ? What are those disgusting shameless clothes ? Hai Allah ! Tell me I am dreaming. Tell me I am in hell.

ISMAAT   Oh God Mum.

ZEENAT: Don't oh God mum me young lady. I am your Ammi.

ISMAAT   Oh Allah Ammi then.

JAMIL   Beti, these clothes are very unsuitable. Your hair is like a giant Tarantula. *(Laughs.)* I'm sorry darling, but you look ridiculous. *(Laughs again.)*

ISMAAT   I am not. This is fashion Dad. You're just too old to appreciate it.

ZEENAT: How will I show my face to Allah ? My own daughter. Dancing, like Shaitan, with a white boy.

ISMAAT   So that's what this is really about. You are upset because I make friends with a white boy ?

ZEENAT   In our people, shareef girls do not have boyfriends. And here you are, in your own home, dressed like that, with a *(With disgust in her voice)* a white man. So pale, so disgusting. Do you know, they don't even wash properly after going to the toilet ? They use paper. Dirty dirty people.

ISMAAT   Mother, Ammi, there is nothing wrong with white skin, or toilet paper for that.

ZEENAT   Hai Allah *(Slaps her chest)*. How will I face my family now ? What will people say ?

ISMAAT   You never understand, neither of you. You don't even try. Who gives a shit what other people say ?

JAMIL: Calm down you two. Shouting at each other is not the answer.

ZEENAT: And you *(She points at Jamil)*, it's all your fault. What kind of a father are you ?

JAMIL: Now Ismaat, we are reasonable parents. We let you wear skirts and go out. We even said you could marry whoever you want, as long as he's a Muslim Punjabi of between 20 and 30 with a good education, preferably a doctor or an engineer, with a good family and who doesn't drink alcohol. Now, isn't that really reasonable ? But this, this is going to far. Dancing with a boy in your own living room.

ISMAAT   All my friends go out and party and drink and have boyfriends. And I will if I want to.

ZEENAT   Hai Allah *(Slaps her chest)*. We have raised the devil's child. She's ruined my life.

ISMAAT You don't need any help from me Ammi, to ruin your life. You've done a great job of it for yourself.
Ismaat exits.

ZEENAT What I want to know is, how are you going to sort out your precious daughter ? Maybe I should start looking for a Rishta.

JAMIL But she's only 17. I want her to go to University. We can't get her married. I want her to have the chances we never did.

ZEENAT What good are those chances without izzat ? What will people say ? That our daughter is awara ?

The doorbell rings. Zeenat exits. Jamil stands for a while. Then he goes over to the Radiogram and puts on the Sex pistols music. He starts to move about and then starts to jump up and down. He is watching himself in the mirror. He makes his hair wild and begins to dance energetically. Zeenat ushers Maulvi Sahib (Played by Jinh) on stage. Eventually Jamil sees the Maulvi and stop dancing. He hastily moves over to the radiogram and switches it off. The radiogram exits.

ZEENAT Maulvi Sahib has come to collect chanda for the Mosque.

JAMIL Maulvi Sahib, I wasn't expecting you so soon. Welcome, salaam a-lekum.

MAULVI   Walekum asalaam.

JAMIL   Come in, come in. Sir. Oh, I see, you are wondering about the music. Well, you see, I believe that to understand the mind of the punks, we have to get inside their heads. This is just research. I always research every thing I am trying to understand.

MAULVI   Everything ?

JAMIL   Well, within reason, you see. Not alcohol, or prostitution, heaven forbid !

MAULVI   These punks have been beating up our boys when they come out of the mosques, terrorising young Asian school children, harassing young mothers. What is there to understand Jamil sahib. They are filth. They are fascists. They are our enemy.

Zeenat brings Ismaat in, trying to cover Ismaat's hair with a dupatta as she does so.

ISMAAT   Salam-a-lekum maulvi sahib.

MAULVI   Walekum asalaam *(Places his hand on her head)*. Jeeti raho, jeeti raho. Masha-Allah, is this the fashion my dear ?

ISMAAT   It's what punks wear.

MAULVI   How is it that our daughter is siding with skinheads and punks, those that frighten and scare your own peoples ?

ISMAAT   Abbuji, maulvi sahib, punks aren't the same as skin heads you know. It's the skinheads beating up all the black kids.

MAULVI   Punks, skin-heads, it is all the same to us dear child. You can dress like them and then they let you in. But an old man like me, it is apparent to all who see me who I am, and all white kids see me in the same way.

ISMAAT   When you talk like that it's just like them.

MAULVI   Who ?

ISMAAT   The racist whites. Saying we're all the same. You saying they're all the same, the goras ?

ZEENAT   Hai allah, what are you saying to maulvi sahib ? And you haven't even covered your head in his presence. Go and change.

MAULVI   It's OK Zeenat behn, your daughter is teaching me tolerance.

JAMIL   Maulvi Sahib, come. I will show you the radishes in the garden. Proper moolis they are. And the Dhaniya is blooming. Come come.

ZEENAT   What is going on in that crazy head of yours ? Are you determined to rub your families name in mud or are you going to start seeing some sense ?

ISMAAT   Don't talk to me as if I'm a child. I'm seventeen. Nearly old enough to vote.

ZEENAT   How can you do this to me ? Oh god what have I done to deserve this hell of a life with this Devil's child !

ISMAAT   I know you never wanted to come here Mum. But I'm not you. I like it here. I'm glad I've come here. But every time I do anything, anything, like playing netball at school, like making white friends, like speaking in English, Mum, you punish me. You punish me because I won't kill myself like you have. You said you would rather die than come here. And that's what you've done. It feels like you're dead!

Lights down. Flashback Voice Over - Gary : "Yes she lives here. This is her flatmate Gary Johnson. Yes she is here, shall I call her? Oh I see... Oh my god, when? Oh no..."
Lights up. Jinh and Rhiannon help Ismaat change into Salwar Kameez.

ISMAAT   Who am I?
I am an Asian woman wearing salwar kameez and dupatta.
If Ammi could see me now.
No more leather jacket and jeans.
We all go back to our roots.
I watched myself in the mirror as I dressed.
I was surprised at how I emerged.
Was I a chameleon ?
Am I still ?
When I grow up I want to be me.

When I grow up I want to be me.
I am grown up, but who am I ?

RHIANNON   You said to your mother that you were glad you had come to this country ?

ISMAAT   I was. When I first found out we were coming I was so excited.

JINH   We have come to the last part of the journey, where you can do whatever is in your heart. It is now your own choice. Ji-hazoor-ha-kaly-aadmi-hain.

There is a flash and a change of scene.
Rhiannon gives Ismaat some white flowers. Jinh gestures for her to turn around. She sees two graves.

ISMAAT   I hate coming here. It is such a desolate place. Look, gravestones all around £99 for a six-by-six by-two foot hole in the ground, 99 years lease. All around here are people like my parents, who came to this country and died. Even in death they are segregated, all the Muslims clustered together. Every time I come here, I feel angry. And then I feel guilty. I go home and I can't swallow food because Mum and Dad are buried under this earth. I can't cope with the warmth in my bed because I think of them, lying in this cold damp ground. No, I am angry. Ammi, Abbu, do you hear me ? I am angry with you. Because you're dead. Because you're gone. I am angry that you died and you left me. I am angry that you made the choices you made and didn't try to protect me. You didn't even know what it would be like. Damn it....

Lights Down. Music - North Indian Classical. Jamil and Zeenat, dressed in white, enter and stand in their "graves". Ismaat screams in fear and hides behind Jinh.

JAMIL   Now that is not what I thought would happen.

ZEENAT   Ismaat, my daughter, come to us. Your crying has brought us down from heaven.

JAMIL   My God, no disrespect sir, but what an utterly terrible place. Quite quite frightening.

ZEENAT   Yes, one one forgets what a terrible place the earth is. Ismaat, my child, Ammi is here for you.

ISMAAT   They're not my parents. Look at them. My mother is smiling. She wouldn't do that. Look at what they're wearing, that's not how my parents would dress.

ZEENAT   Yes I know, the white is terribly boring. But we have to follow the paradisiacal rules outside of Janat, visiting loved ones and all that. Strict code of dress so as not to shock earthlings pyari.

JAMIL   Yes, I must say I've lost all desire to wear clothes in the last few years.

ISMAAT   What ? You mean you and Ammi don't wear any clothes in Janat ?

ZEENAT   We are not naked pyari beti. We have no bodies. We are spiritual beings. We do not exist as physical entities. Now, come to Ammi.

Ismaat walks nearer and then stops a few steps away from Zeenat.

ISMAAT   When I was a kid I felt like you were frozen. Suspended, not there, always hurting. You never held me, or hugged me, or kissed me.

ZEENAT   I was afraid of touching because I was numb inside.

ISMAAT   I felt like you just gave up.

ZEENAT   In a way I did. After I watched mother die it felt like I had died too. So many friends and loved ones, dead. I was only a child. I never managed to leave it behind me. You are right, I did give up.

ISMAAT   You never talked to me about your life before. You never told me anything.

ZEENAT   When I was fifteen I was playing out, in secret as I was too old to be out by then. I was up a tree. I was called in. I didn't know what was happening. There were people I didn't know in the house, men, women, a maulvi. Next minute they're covering my head with a red dupatta and the maulvi is saying the three words to me.

ISMAAT   The three words.

ZEENAT   Yes to marriage. I didn't know who the man was. I didn't even say yes. Girls didn't always say it. Their silence was taken as an affirmation.

ISMAAT   You should have shouted no.

ZEENAT   And stayed where I was ? Your father was a good man. I wouldn't have got a better match.

ISMAAT   There are lots of good men around, it doesn't mean you have to marry them.

ZEENAT   They took me to their house. For three years I served his family... cooking, cleaning, working all the time to prove my worth to them. I stopped playing, day-dreaming, singing. I became the perfect daughter in law. But, when you were born all the sister-in-laws gathered around to help. For the first three months I didn't have to lift a finger. At night, someone would bring you to my breast, another one would walk you around until you slept. Antiji would rub my feet, my legs, my shoulders, my head to bring me comfort. I no longer had to do housework, that was the job of the younger women, the ones without children. It was the first and only place in my life where I had some support, some love around me. And then, we came here. Cold, alone. I was not used to living alone, just with you and Jamil. It felt so unnatural.

ISMAAT   You know something Ammi ? When we were leaving and we were at the airport and all our family was there. Do you remember ? Naniji, Beji, Chachi, everyone. I couldn't understand why everyone was crying. That day, at the airport. I remember seeing the red earth. I don't know why but I suddenly felt really upset. I bent down to pick some up and put it in my pocket.

ZEENAT   I remember that. You ruined your clothes.

ISMAAT   I only remembered it years later. When I went to Greece. As soon as I saw the red earth I was so upset. I just wanted you to know Ammi. It hurt me too.

ZEENAT   I couldn't be what you needed. That made it worse. I tried to give you more choices than I had had. But the more choices you had the greater the rift between us. My life and your life are as different as my life and my mother's.

Zeenat and Ismaat embrace. Ismaat gives her mother the white flowers.

ISMAAT   Abbu.

JAMIL   Beti.

They hug.

JAMIL   Now, what did you want to talk to me about ? We have little time left.

ISMAAT   I want to play a game of chess with you..

A chess set appears.

JAMIL   I remember your little tricks beti. You always used to bring out the competitor in me. But now I am in Janat, these earthly pursuits no longer interest me.

ISMAAT   I'll believe that when I see it. *(Moves a piece on the chess board.)* Your move.

Jamil moves a piece distractedly. Ismaat moves another piece. For a few moments they become engrossed in the game. Moving pieces quite rapidly.

JAMIL   How did you do that ?

ISMAAT   Concentration. You taught me that. Remember ?

JAMIL   In India, where chess was first invented, in Moghul times, they used to play with real live pieces, people on horses, in huge courtyards.

ISMAAT   I never learnt much about India before the British raj. We never learnt anything about it in school. I can't imagine that it really existed.

JAMIL   Do you remember that film we watched together, "The Chess Players" ?

ISMAAT   By Satyajit Ray ? Yes I do. The Indian people were so laid back, chilled out. Spending long hot afternoons playing chess. They didn't even notice that the British had moved in. You know, you were a lot like those Indian men in the film.

JAMIL   How?

ISMAAT   You were so in awe of the British, the goras. Those letters you sent back home. You said this place is amazing. You said children get pocket money from the government!

JAMIL   I was talking about family allowance.

ISMAAT   You said they even wash the buses every week.

JAMIL   Did I say that?

ISMAAT   The first London bus we sat on was so grimy you couldn't see out of the windows.

JAMIL   It had been snowing.

ISMAAT   You said the education system was great. But the kids of my age were years behind me in most subjects. You said everything here was fair, people were equal.

JAMIL   I was trying to make it sound exciting but it wasn't all lies. In the post war years in the UK people believed in a just society.

ISMAAT   Not for black people though Dad.

JAMIL   No, not for us.

ISMAAT   When I was growing up in Riverside, there were so many times I wanted you to be angry. But you were always so calm, so accepting.

JAMIL   Perhaps you're right. Do you remember the woman next door?

ISMAAT   The one who complained about the smell of curries ?

JAMIL   And then we saw on television how to cook a curry without the smells escaping, baked in the oven, baked in the oven not cooked on the stove, covered tightly to stop the aromas escaping. But the smell of a curry can't hide.

ISMAAT   Now its balti houses everywhere. You can even buy curries in Cowbridge.

JAMIL   Those days were strange.

ISMAAT   You shouldn't have forced Ammi. You shouldn't have made her come here. It wasn't fair Dad.

JAMIL   I was trying to do the best. For you, for her, for us. I tried to do my best.

ISMAAT   Well, that's check mate.

JAMIL   I taught you well my daughter.

ISMAAT   Abbu, will you do one thing for me before you have to go ?

JAMIL   Name it.

ISMAAT   Tell me the end of the elephant story.

JAMIL   The elephant story, the two hathis who were sathis.

ISMAAT   I never got to hear the end. They had gone wandering, in search of a better home, a better life.

ISMAAT   They travelled all over the world, meeting magical beings, having amazing adventures, having exciting things happen to them...

Jinh and Rhiannon enter in Elephant masks. Music - "A Meeting By The River" by V.M. Bhatt and Ry Cooder.

JAMIL   Big Elephant and Little Elephant...
One day, they were strolling in an unfamiliar jungle. The big elephant tripped and fell, hurting his trunk. He lay there and cried because he was in so much pain. The little elephant nursed the big elephant all night long. She put a cool flannel on the big elephants trunk and bathed it in soothing oils and she sang to the big elephant to make him feel better, but the big elephant was still in pain. All night long the little elephant was afraid, afraid of the dark, afraid of being alone, afraid of the moonlight, afraid of the night owl, afraid of the shadows, afraid of the wind, afraid of the big elephants' pain, afraid of the future. By the time dawn came

the little elephant had exhausted herself from fear. She was so tired she could hardly keep herself awake. She slept and she dreamed. *(Jinh and Rhiannon take their masks off. Rhiannon puts her mask on Ismaat.)* She dreamed of an ocean which was large and blue and deep. She dreamed of a golden sandy beach. She dreamed of waves breaking on the golden sand. She dreamed of night and day and the moon and the stars and the sun. She dreamed of life and death. She dreamed of new and old. When she awoke, many hours later, she forgot where she had been the night before. The terror had gone. The place she lay was bathed in a warm, blissful sunshine. Little elephant yawned and stretched and she stirred and slowly rose thinking of breakfast. Coffee and toast and orange juice and fried eggs. Mmmm. But, as she rose with her mouth salivating the terror of the night before came back and she remembered big elephant's pain. But when little elephant turned to look to see how big elephant was, she could not find him. Big elephant had gone. She looked around but big elephant was nowhere to be seen. Little elephant was beside herself with worry and grief. Tears fell from her eyes and they fell onto the ground and they rolled down the hill where they started to collect and grow until they had formed a puddle... *(Jamil, Zeenat, Jinh and Rhiannon take water-silks and enact the following)* and still little elephant carried on crying and her tears collected and the puddle grew into a pond and it kept growing until it had become a lake full of salt water. Still the little elephant continued to cry until the lake grew and it grew until it had become so large that it had become an ocean. And little elephant's sobs spread over the ocean making it move and roll with waves breaking on the edge and suddenly, little elephant stopped crying and she looked around herself and she saw the ocean and the waves breaking on a golden shore and the moon and the stars and the sun in the sky and she realised that her dream from the night before had come true. And she knew that big elephant had not gone from her because big elephant would always be in her heart. Her search had come to an end because her world had always been in her heart and not somewhere else as she had thought. So, the little elephant stopped searching and she stayed where she was for wherever she was, was home.

Ismaat has fallen asleep.

JAMIL   Good Night...

ZEENAT   Shab bakhair.

JINH   Soja.

RHIANNON   Nos Da.

Ismaat is left alone on stage. Music continues to play. Video images of modern "multi-cultural" Cardiff.

Black out. Silence.
The End.

Glossary

Aata	Chapatti Flour
Abbu	Dad
Allah	God
Ammi	Mum
Ankhen band	Eyes closed
Angrezi	English
Array	Hey
Begum	Respectful title for a woman
Beji	Mother / Grandmother
Beti	Daughter
Bhai	Brother
Bunder	Monkey
Chacli	Aunt
Chanda	Donation
Chappal	Sandal
Choti memsahib	Little madam
Chup karo	Be quiet
Dhaniya	Corriander
Eid	Muslim religious festival
Farangi	Non-believer
Gora	White
Hathi	Elephant
Hai allah	Oh god
Haya	Shyness
Hum tumharay pagal	I am crazy about you
Hut paray	Get away
Heer	A legendary heroine from 'Heer Ranjha'
Izzat	Respect/honour
Jeeti raho	Have a long life

Kaan band	Ears closed
Kahan say Aaee ho	Where are you from
Kala	Black
Khilona jan kar tum to mera dil tor jatay ho	
	You break my heart as if I was a toy
Kismet	Destiny
Maan ki zabaan	Mother tongue
Masti	Naughtiness
Masha allah	By the grace of god
Memsahib	Madam
Moti	Fat
Mussafar	Traveller
Naak band	Nose closed
Naniji	Maternal Grandmother
Pagal	Mad
Pagla	Crazy man
Paneer	Indian Cheese
Reshum	Silk
Saathi	Mate
Safar	Journey
Salam-a-lekum	Muslim greeting
Shab bakhair	Good evening
Shaitan	Devil
Salan	Curry sauce
Sharam	Shame
Shareef	Good/ Well behaved/ Moral
Sarson ka saag	Spinach
Walekum asalam	Response to Salam-a-lekum
Waqt	Time

Shireen Shah, Brigitta Roy.
Rehearsal, Summer 1996.

photo: Amy Nicholls

Shireen Shah, Brigitta Roy, Shiv Grewal.   *photo: Amy Nicholls*

Safar

Mother Tongue

The language which was mine, here it has gone
I can't speak to my mother without my mother tongue
All around me are people who belong
I am alone, don't even know where I'm from
Even the ocean tires of carving rock and stone
Will these blooded shores ever be my home

یہ جو زباں

یہ جو زباں میری تھی میری یہاں نہیں
ماں سے کیسے بات کہ ماں کی زباں نہیں

اس پاس کوئ ہیں یہ گھر والے نہیں
میں گھر کہاں ہو بس یہ پتا نہیں

کیا ہی ہیں کیا ہن گئی بھی سے نہ پوچھ
ایں بدل گئی ہوں کہ کوئ نشاں نہیں

کاٹ کاٹ پتھروں کو بھر تھک گئی
اس خون کے دیا میں اپنا جہاں نہیں

Samia Malik

Gulp
by Roger Williams

Gulp was premiéred by the Made in Wales Stage Company at Chapter Arts Centre, Cardiff, in July 1997 with the following cast.

Rob	Keiron Self
Susie	Lowri Mae
Mark	Roland Powell
Luke	Oliver Ryan
Steven	Greg Ashton

All are in their early twenties
The play is set in and around present-day Cardiff

Directed by	Jeff Teare
Designer	Carolyn Willitts
Lighting Designer	Paul Taylor
Assistant director	Rebecca Gould

This version of the play was staged in October 1997 at Chapter, Cardiff, & St.Andrew's Lane Theatre, Dublin, with James Westaway as Luke and Ceris Jones as Steven.

Directed by Rebecca Gould

Gulp

Act One

1. *Darkness. Andrea True Connection's 'More, More, More' begins to play, and disco lights rise front of stage. Susie comes forward and self-consciously starts to dance to the music. She is dressed in standard club wear and is a little drunk. Embarrassed, she stops, gestures to the audience that she doesn't want to be up on stage doing this, hides her face, before taking a deep breath and carrying on. She starts to mime to the main vocal when it begins, but after a few words, stops, regains her composure and starts to mime once more. From here on in she builds in confidence and starts to perform more convincingly; dancing and miming.*

As the second verse begins Rob and Steven appear on stage and join Susie to start singing the backing vocals. To begin with they are also quite self-conscious but as the song plays on they grow in confidence until all three end up performing the same dance steps as though they had rehearsed the routine.

The applause and cheers of an audience take over from the music as the song fades. Susie, Rob and Steven take their curtain call and the lights fade away.

The sound of the sea crashing against the shore takes over from the sound of applause and carries over into the next scene.

2. *A light picks out Steven standing alone.*

STEVEN
There are no hard and fast rules when it comes to building a raft. There is no right or wrong way to go about it. In fact, anything that is flat, floats, and holds the weight of one person could quite legitimately be called a raft.

A raft is carried along by the tide. It relies upon the constant pulse of the water to move along. There is no steering wheel, no road map. It is guided by the waves; reaching outwards to steady it, to lead it in the right direction, to bring it home.

Sound of waves fades.

Gulp

3. *As one light fades another rises to pick out Susie.*

SUSIE   I've always known that I was going to be famous. I've always had this extra special feeling about it right down in the pit of my stomach. To be honest I knew way back in nineteen eighty three that I was going to be big. I saw it all. In a vision.

I was lying on my bed when it happened, watching *The Kids from Fame* on the colour portable Mum and Dad had given me for Christmas, open-mouthed, enthralled.

It was the episode when the college play was in danger of being abandoned because the teachers, against the wishes of Mr Shorofsky, had gone on strike. The students had been planning an all-singing, all-dancing, production of *Othello* and things were looking bleak until Bruno, Co-Co, and Leroy saved the day.

It was a classic episode, but it wasn't until they launched into their final big number that I experienced this overwhelming sensation. A blinding light struck me, I felt faint, and as the music roared on, 'Desda, Desda, Desdemona,' I could hear someone cheering my name and my sight blurred momentarily. As it cleared though, I looked back at the tv and saw myself up there behind the screen alongside the actors. I was there, singing, dancing, taking my curtain call before a riotous standing ovation. Fame, I thought. I'm going to live forever.

4. *As one light fades another picks out Rob.*

ROB   I was eleven years old when I first fell in love. His name was Marcus and he was the swimming instructor at our local pool. Tall, broad, brownish-blonde, with deep green eyes, Marcus was the most beautiful eighteen-year-old I had ever seen, and by the final lesson, as I peered over at him through my misty goggles, I was convinced that we were made for one another.

I loved everything about him, especially the way his hair flopped over his eyes when he looked down into the water, and the leather bracelets he used to wear around his wrists, like Morton from A-ha. He was wonderful. So wonderful, in fact, that I signed up for another course of lessons in the autumn even though my crawl was by far the best in the class and my back-stroke miles ahead of anyone else's.

But on the morning of the first lesson, as I stood waiting for Marcus by the pool side in my brand-new swimming trunks, Julie, a frumpy pretender to Marcus's throne, appeared and announced that she was our new teacher. Marcus had gone away to college. I'd been dumped.

I'm convinced that I never really recovered from the blow. Boyfriends two through till five were unremarkable in comparison. Quick fumbles at the roller disco. Names I've long forgotten.

Boyfriend number six was the first man I ever got to snog though, and it was everything a good snog should be. Determined, firm, and well controlled, without excessive saliva or dribbling.

Relationships seven to thirteen were also mostly uneventful so I won't bore you with the details, although number fourteen gets a mention for buying me a Rolex, a CD-player, and a Carnival

Soda Stream.

Fifteen through till twenty-one I don't really remember much about, except that number eighteen had very bad breath, and nineteen used to keep a pet lizard on a shelf in his mother's airing cupboard. Twenty-two had a thing about stockings, and number twenty-three gets a credit for being the proud owner of the biggest dick I have ever had the pleasure of coming across. Weighing in at a foot long, and at least two inches thick. Honestly.

After King Kong I lose count. To be fair, nobody else stood a chance in comparison. There were men all over the place, and the relationships I had lasted anything from three minutes to two months. I kept staggering on, hoping, praying, that one day I'd open a door, turn a corner, open my eyes, and find Marcus standing there waiting for me, wearing the tightest pair of lycra swimming shorts ever invented. It never happened. But I did meet Steven.

5. *A large bathroom. Night. There is one door, a bath, sink, toilet, cabinet, chair and clothes horse dressed with damp washing. There is a big window to one side partly covered by an inadequate curtain. Rob is looking into the mirror styling his hair with gel. Susie appears a moment later dressed up for a night out and ready to go. She watches Rob getting ready and leans against the door frame.*

SUSIE   'Dear Denise. I need your advice. I'm a young, wickedly beautiful woman sharing a flat with a fairly good-looking twenty four year old man and his receding hairline. There's nothing sexual about our relationship, unfortunately, but he's my friend, and he needs help. Quick. You see, he's depressed, not slit your wrists depressed, just boring, he's turned boring on me. He's stopped going out, he's lost all interest in enjoying himself, and since I'm such a caring, wonderful, kind friend I want to sort him out. I've tried talking to him. I've suggested he seeks professional therapy, chocolate, or a course of hot safe sex with a stranger, but he doesn't want to know. What else can I do? Please help. Troubled Susie of Cardiff.'

ROB   Funny.

SUSIE   I thought so. *(Beat)* Aren't you ready yet?

ROB   Five more minutes.

SUSIE   That's what you said half an hour ago.

ROB   What's the problem? You want me to look gorgeous,

don't you?

SUSIE   Yeah, but I'm not a miracle worker Rob.

ROB *(Forced)* Ha. Ha.

SUSIE   It's for your own good mun. I'm saving you.

ROB   Saving me? From what?

SUSIE   Boring middle age. A fate worse than castration. I'm sorry, but you just can't stop going out on Saturday nights Rob. It isn't allowed. You're twenty-four, you're a pretty young boy, you should be out there, dancing, drinking, waving your arms in the air like you just don't care.

ROB   Who says?

SUSIE   I'm sure it's your hormones. One minute you're tearing up the dance floor to Rozalla, and the next you're stopping in with the remote control and your lottery ticket. It's not natural.

ROB   Not everybody likes going out on Saturday nights Susie.

SUSIE   And thank God they don't! The queue for the toilets'd be horrific and you'd never get served at the bar. Talking of which - we'd better get a move on.

ROB   All right, all right. I'll come quietly.

SUSIE   That'll be a first.

ROB   Oh. Excuse me while I wet myself.

SUSIE   Come on, you're going to enjoy yourself. I'm going to make sure of it. And you never know, you might strike lucky.

ROB   No ta. Didn't I tell you I've declared kissing unhygienic?

SUSIE   You might get tempted.

ROB   About as likely as you staying sober.

SUSIE   Hey! I can hold my drink.

ROB   Yeah. With both your hands when you're not dancing.

SUSIE   Don't worry. I'm not talking love here Rob. I'm talking y'know, bedroom, underpants, ky jelly, orgasm! And you can't tell me that you don't want to have an orgasm.

ROB   Not with anyone else in the room, no, I don't.

SUSIE   I give up.

ROB   Good.

SUSIE   It's pathetic. How long has it been since you and pig face split up?

ROB   Give it a rest Susie.

SUSIE   No. Come on. How long has it been?

ROB   Can't remember, don't want to.

SUSIE   Yes you do. What is it? Five? Six months?

ROB   Way out.

SUSIE   What then?

ROB   Almost nine months if you've got to put a figure on it.

SUSIE   And you still haven't got over him? That's sick.

ROB   If you say so.

SUSIE   You can't carry on like this Rob. You've got to find someone else.

ROB   Why? What are you going to do about it if I don't? Arrest me?

SUSIE   Steven wasn't perfect Rob.

ROB   I know he wasn't. Genesis and Dire Straits were his favourite bands for God's sake.

SUSIE   So let go. Forget about him.

ROB   I can't. I don't want to.

SUSIE   After nine months I don't think you've got a lot of choice. You don't need him Rob.

ROB   No. But that doesn't stop me wanting him, does it?

SUSIE   You're a lost cause.

Rob pulls his jacket on.

ROB   Very probably. But what about you? Haven't you got another candidate in your sights?

SUSIE   Robert bach. I never stop looking. Every day a new possibility opens up.

ROB   And so do your legs?

SUSIE   Exactly. So what're we waiting for?

Exit.

6. *Another light picks out Mark standing alone.*

MARK   The first time I decided to take the jump I spent nearly three hours getting ready. And two baths, one wet shave, and a brand new pair of pants later, I managed to make it as far as the front door before chickening out and deciding to stay in.

The second time I talked myself into going. I actually managed to make it as far as the bus stop, but as the bus wound its way into town I found myself listing all the reasons why going through with it wasn't such a good idea, and didn't bother getting off at the stop.

A few weeks later I tried again. And with a considerable amount of Southern Comfort inside me I made it as far as the road, then the door, and I even stepped inside once before panicking, deciding that it really wasn't such a clever idea after all and heading home.

Tonight's the night though. It's got to be. It's going to happen tonight. I've decided that I'm going to walk in, buy a drink, and stay there until somebody, fair or foul, romeo or letch, comes along and makes a move. It's going to happen. I'm determined that before the end of the night I'm going to be standing against a wall, pressed up against someone, with my heart pounding and my imagination racing. My tongue'll be jammed between his lips, and he's going to slip his warm, unfamiliar hand past the waist band of my trousers, deep down into my jockey shorts, and beyond. *(Beat)* Fingers crossed.

7. *The men's toilets at a night-club. We can hear the muffled sound of dance music outside. Rob is sitting, fully dressed, on a toilet with his head in his hands and the cubicle door wide open. Susie enters a moment later with a drink.*

SUSIE   You all right?

Rob splutters.

SUSIE   No, didn't think you were.

Susie rests her bag up on the sink unit, and checks her appearance in the mirror.

ROB   I'm never going to drink again.

SUSIE   Wise words. Shame I don't believe you.

ROB   I feel like shit.

SUSIE   Look like it too if you don't mind me saying.

ROB   Cheers.

SUSIE   You're welcome. *(Beat)* Well? Tell me. Was I right or was I right?

ROB   About what?

SUSIE   Christopher. Gorgeous, isn't he? I'd give him eight out of ten.

ROB   You never were very good at maths though were you?

SUSIE   He likes you.

ROB   Does he?

SUSIE   Can't you tell? *(Beat)* He's a teacher.

ROB   *(Going over to the sink to splash water on his face.)* That's nice.

SUSIE   And he's got his own house, a new car, and one of the others has made it very clear, in no uncertain terms, that he's hung like a donkey.

ROB   Do we know that for sure Susie?

SUSIE   No, but it'll be fun finding out whether they're lying or not. *(Beat)* Well?

ROB   Well what?

SUSIE   Good God Rob, catch up will you? D'you like him?

ROB   Not particularly.

SUSIE   He doesn't mind that you've been sick. He thinks it's sweet.

ROB   Sweet?

SUSIE   I told him you were feeling nervous. Well, I actually said you were a little bit anxious about meeting him for the first time and that the chunder monster had paid a visit.

ROB   For God's sake Susie!

SUSIE   What? He's nice.

ROB   Yeah well, I can do without bastard nice tonight thanks.

SUSIE   I thought you'd be chuffed.

ROB   Think again.

SUSIE   So, you don't like him then?

ROB   Congratulations.

SUSIE   But what's wrong with him?

ROB   Where d'you want me to start?

SUSIE   What? You're not interested at all? Not even a tiny bit? But he's good-looking, well-dressed and he's got a gorgeous body. I swear to God, if he wasn't a poofter I'd have him in ten seconds flat.

ROB   I don't doubt it.

SUSIE   So why don't you go home with him then? Talk to him. Get to know him. It isn't as though you'd have to take your clothes off or anything is it?

Rob glares at her.

SUSIE   Don't tell me you're swapping sides all of a sudden.

ROB   Susie, all I want to do tonight is go home and go to bed.

SUSIE   Alone?

ROB   Yes thank you.

SUSIE   Pervert.

ROB   That's what they tell me.

SUSIE   You've got a nice bloke out there Rob. Tall, broad, good looking, ok, I'll grant you he's got wonky teeth, but he's not that bad, when his mouth's closed. Oh, go on Rob. Do it for me.

ROB   Do it yourself.

SUSIE   Please.

ROB   Are you getting commission for this?

SUSIE   Well you can't say he never offered.

ROB   I know. It's just...

SUSIE   Steven? God you need help boy.

ROB   Probably. But I don't need it from him.

She heads for the door.

SUSIE   Well, I'd better go and put the poor bloke out of his misery then. He's been standing outside that cloakroom for the last half hour, biting his lip, wondering whether his luck's in.

ROB   Tell him I'm ill.

SUSIE   Better not. He'd want to come home and nurse you better. God knows he's probably got the uniform and everything.

ROB   Susie, can we go back to the flat then please? I really have had enough. So when you've finished, can we go?

SUSIE   Yeah yeah. I don't know why you like coming to this dump anyway.

Susie exits. Pause. Rob looks into the mirror again, splashes some water over his face and unbuttons his top shirt buttons. He spots Susie's handbag on the counter and begins to look through it. He pulls out a red handkerchief, a mirror, some condoms, a bar of chocolate, a small screw driver, and then a pair of women's knickers. As he lifts out the last item Mark walks in. He is flustered, closes the door tightly and presses his back up against it. They are almost instantly aware of each other's presence, turn, and face one another.

ROB   Hi.

Rob remembers the women's underwear he is holding.

ROB   I'm looking after them for someone. For a friend. A female friend. She'll be back in a minute. She's just gone outside to tell a man that I'm not interested. But these have got nothing to do with me. Obviously. I mean, I'm not into that sort of thing. But that's not to say I disapprove of anyone who is though. I mean, each to their own really, isn't it?

Mark smiles, goes over to the sink and runs his hand under the tap. He is bleeding a little.

ROB   Ouch.

MARK   It's nothing. Caught it against some broken glass at the bar.

ROB   You should sue.

Rob offers Susie's handkerchief to him.

ROB   Here.

MARK   Thanks.

He wraps it around the cut.

ROB   So what happened?   Did you pass comment on the barman's new hair-cut and he pulled a bottle on you?

MARK   It's my own stupid fault. I wasn't paying attention. I get a bit nervous when I come to places like this.

ROB   So why d'you bother?

MARK   Ah, y'know.....

ROB   Don't worry.   Everyone's here for much the same reason. I can fix you up with an eager to learn Geography teacher with funny front teeth and a quiff if you're interested?

MARK   Front teeth?

ROB   Doesn't matter.

MARK   I'm just not very good at it.   I can be talking away to someone at the bar, and everything's going fine, it's all running along nicely when, for no reason whatsoever, I panic, and balls it up.

ROB   Occupational hazard.

MARK   Someone must be watching me, following my every move, waiting to chuck the spanner in at the right moment.

ROB   What went wrong?

MARK   Another disaster. I met someone. We were getting along great, I think. At least, he was looking me straight in the eye, y'know the way you do when you're interested? And I was trying to keep calm, not get too hopeful, when I just knocked my arm against my glass like that.... *(Demonstrates.)* And....

ROB   Shit.

MARK   Doesn't make a very good first impression does it really?

ROB   Worse things have happened.

MARK   Tell me about it. I must be jinxed.

ROB   Still bleeding?

MARK   Little bit.

He moves to give the handkerchief back.

ROB   Nah, keep it. It's my flat-mate's. She won't miss it.

MARK   *(Pointing to the knickers.)* Are those hers too?

ROB   Ah yes. She'll be back in a minute, she's just gone to break some bad news.

MARK   To your unwanted admirer?

ROB   She takes more interest in my love life than she does her own.

MARK   Sounds like I could do with her services.

The door swings open and Susie rushes back in. She spots her hand bag.

SUSIE   Thank God. I thought I'd lost it. You know how it is when you can't find something? Your keys, or your purse, or something? Your heart starts pounding doesn't it? And your head's buzzing? What an amazing feeling! I've been running round like a mad cow trying to find it for the last five minutes. Cheapest drug I know.

ROB   Did you talk to him?

SUSIE   Yeah. He sends his sympathies.

ROB   You what?

SUSIE   I told him your auntie'd died.

ROB   Susie!

SUSIE   It's all right, I said you were close.

ROB   You are such a liar.

SUSIE   I know.   Anyway, I just came back to fetch my bag and tell you that a few of us are going on somewhere else now, so don't wait up eh, I'll see you tomorrow.

ROB   Susie!

SUSIE   What? You've got the cab fare haven't you?

ROB   Yes.

SUSIE   So?

ROB   So, I thought we were going home together.   Now?

SUSIE   Relax Rob.   You'll be fine.   Just don't tell the taxi driver you've been chucking up like a trooper all night or he won't let you anywhere near his back seat ok?

ROB   Susie.

SUSIE   *(To Mark.)*   Sorry, he gets like this.   Time of the month.

ROB   I'm not happy Susie.

SUSIE   *(To Mark.)*   See what I mean?

ROB   Look, you can't promise to do one thing and then change your mind just like that.   We're supposed to be friends.

SUSIE   Whatever gave you that idea?

ROB   Susie!

SUSIE   Oh, calm down before you rupture yourself. It's not the end of the world. You'll be all right, and anyway you seem to have made another new friend in here tonight, tucked away inside the gents, very cosy. *(To Mark)* Hello there.

MARK   Hi.

SUSIE   So you won't be needing me anymore will you? Take this one home. He looks nice. Bend his ear about how horrible I am. Tell him how I keep abusing our friendship. *(To Mark)* It's a long sick story. *(To Rob)* But however much you scream and shout and stamp your feet, I refuse to feel guilty, you should know by now that I don't have a conscience.

ROB   Just don't make a noise when you come in then, ok?

SUSIE   *(Shouting as she leaves the room.)* Don't worry. I'll be as quiet as a mouse. Promise.

Susie leaves. The two men look at one another blankly.

8. *Sound of waves crashing against the shore. Lights rise on Steven standing alone.*

STEVEN   In time you will learn to trust the raft. You will begin to understand its movements and appreciate its capabilities. You will start to read the way it rides, until eventually, the raft becomes yours.

9. *Lights rise on a small domestic kitchen later that night. It is bright, colourful and compact. There are posters plastered across the walls. A student kitchen maybe. Mark is sitting at the table with a mug of coffee. Rob enters with a small box of plasters a moment later and gives it to Mark.*

ROB   There you go.

MARK   Ta.

ROB   I knew we had some somewhere. But finding stuff in this place gets a bit difficult after a while when you live with a woman who doesn't understand the concept of tidiness.

MARK   It's just the two of you living here then?

ROB   Yep, like an old married couple.

MARK   And you get on? No arguments?

ROB   God yeah, plenty. We've had stand-up rows in the hallway about whose turn it was to take the rubbish out before now.

MARK   But you haven't killed her yet?

ROB   I've come close.

MARK   I used to live with someone, but well, it didn't work out.

Mark has failed to open the plaster. Rob does it for him. Embarrassed pause.

MARK   Have you known Susie long?

ROB   My ex-boyfriend introduced us. He went to school with her, they were good friends for a long time.

MARK   *Were* good friends?

ROB   He got the Playstation, and I got Susie. It was part of the divorce settlement. Someone had to have her, and well, after many bitter rows, I won custody. Have you seen *Kramer Versus Kramer?*

MARK   Nasty was it?

ROB   Nastier.

MARK   And Susie sided with you?

ROB   She took the break-up worse than I did really. From her reaction you'd swear she'd do Steve in with the bread knife if he ever showed his face round here again.

MARK   She looks after you, doesn't she?

ROB   She likes to think so.

MARK   Like tonight?

ROB   She's very good when it comes to warding off evil spirits.

MARK   What does she do?

ROB   She sings. Well, she'd like to sing. She'd love to start singing her own songs one day, if anyone'd stay in the room long enough to listen. What she actually does is mime. She impersonates famous singers in clubs, pubs, hotels, wherever she can get the work really. But she goes the whole hog. She'll select a singer, work on the act for ages, study the songs, the moves, and get the look together. Wig, make-up, sequinned dress, shoulder pads, the full works. Let's see, she's been Kate Bush, Shirley Bassey, Tina Turner...

MARK   And she really looks like them?

ROB   Not close up no. Her Karen Carpenter was good. Scary really. But Karen's been a bit of a sore point since she was dropped from the act.

MARK   Why? What happened?

ROB   Too many doughnuts basically. She was going through a nasty break-up with what was at the time the love-of-her-life, and started comfort eating. Danish pastries, cheesy Quavers. She put on so much weight that she just wasn't convincing when she did Karen Carpenter after that. She went from being Karen's twin to looking sod all like her.

MARK   Seriously?

ROB   Yeah. When she realized it wasn't working anymore she threw away the costume, wig, backing tape, the lot, and started doing Alison Moyet instead. She'd probably have given you a quick demonstration tonight if she hadn't been so desperate to get off. She loves an audience.

MARK   Why was she in such a hurry anyway?

ROB   God knows. But there's probably a man involved. It's amazing. She's the only straight woman I know who can walk into a club full of gay men and pull.

MARK   Sounds like she could give me a few tips.

ROB   She calls it girl power.

MARK   I could do with some whatever it is.

ROB   You can't be that desperate?

MARK   No? You'd be shocked. I'm twenty-six and still single.

ROB   You're not missing much.

MARK   Twenty-six though.

ROB   Twenty-six nothing. If you haven't found anyone to settle down with by the time you're forty, forty-five, that's when you want to start worrying, that's when you want put an advert in the papers.

MARK   Just a date would be nice at the moment.

ROB   Why? When was the last time you went out with a man?

MARK   You want an exact figure? Try never.

ROB   Never?

MARK   Yep, and never will at this rate.

ROB   What? You've never been out with anyone? You're kidding?

MARK   Sick isn't it? I'm twenty-six and still trying to pull.

ROB   What? You haven't had a relationship at all?

MARK   Sad but true.

ROB   Not one? Not even a kiss?

MARK   I told you earlier. I start chatting someone up and before I get to know more than their Christian name, I mess it up, and they make their escape.

ROB   But you must've been out with someone, a man?

MARK   Not yet.

ROB   Why? How long have you been looking?

MARK   A year. Eighteen months.

ROB   And still no luck? But you have come out?

MARK   To some people yeah. My flat-mate.

ROB   And?

MARK   He left. I just don't understand where I'm going wrong. I mean, what's the matter with me? Why do I keep blowing it?

ROB   You're asking me?

MARK   You've had boyfriends haven't you?

ROB   Well, yeah.

MARK   Lots?

ROB   You could say I've had a few.

MARK   So where am I going wrong then? What's my problem?

ROB   You just have to keep looking, I suppose.

MARK   But I'm always looking, I never stop looking. I'm in the supermarket and I look sideways at the man pushing the trolley past me and I think, is he, could we? I'm supposed to be working at my computer in the office and I find myself staring at all the other guys in the room, wondering what they'd look like without their tailored suits and crisp white shirts. I spend hours thinking about whether they might be up for it, and how I'd go about finding out. It's driving me crazy. *(Pause)* I don't suppose you know of anyone do you? You couldn't, y'know, introduce me to someone?

ROB   What? You want me to fix you up?

MARK   If you don't then it's not a problem, I mean, I just thought I'd ask. On the off-chance more than anything.

ROB   Well. I don't know. What're you looking for?

MARK   A man. Any man.

ROB   A gay man?

MARK   Obviously.

ROB   Not necessarily. Some of us like a challenge.

MARK   No. It can't be difficult. There mustn't be any obstacles. I need a clear run. All I want is a man. An ordinary, standard man. With a tongue, two legs, and a pair of hands. If he can speak English, tie his shoelaces, and spell his own name it'll be a bonus.

ROB   You're not fussy are you?

MARK   I just want a standard guy, someone down to earth, nice. Someone who'll listen to what I actually have to say for myself, someone that'll let me witter on, laugh at my crap jokes, and enjoy spending time with me. Someone like you. Someone nice, ordinary, beautiful..... like you. *(Pause)* Look, I'm sorry. I just thought you might know of someone that's all. I'd better go. But I meant it, what I said, I think. Sorry. I should leave.

Mark stands, and begins to pull his coat on.

ROB   You don't have to.

MARK   No, I should. It's late, and well, I start talking see, and say something, like now, and end up embarrassing everyone. I'm sorry.

ROB   Mark. You didn't embarrass me.

MARK   No? So why do I feel so stupid?

Pause.

ROB   Look. D'you fancy coming out some time? To see Susie's act maybe?

MARK   Well, yeah, I wouldn't mind. When?

Rob gets up and goes to the doorway where Mark is now standing.

ROB   Soon. I could call you.

MARK   Right, well, you'll need my phone number then. D'you want to write it down?

ROB   It's alright. I'll remember.

MARK   Really? Ok, well it's six, five, six...

Rob kisses Mark.

MARK   Seven... *(Beat)* This is usually where I put my foot in it?

ROB   Is it?

MARK   Yeah.

They kiss again, longer this time.

10. *The sound of the sea crashing against the shore wells up and continues. Lights rise on Steven standing alone.*

STEVEN   Balance is the most important principle. You must not rock the raft or disturb the water in any way. It is important that you sit still, remain steady, and concentrate on the raft in progress.

Lights rise on Rob and Mark elsewhere. They stand facing one another, looking each other straight in the eyes and begin to undress each other slowly.

The best way to ride the raft is to sit in the very middle with your arms wrapped around each other, respecting the raft's confines, its edges. Hold on to each other tightly, concentrating your joint weight at the centre, remembering that by maintaining your balance and posture the raft will look after you. It will move you along, steadily, safely.

Fades.

11. *Bathroom. Morning. Mark is sitting in the bath washing. The door bursts open and Susie strides in and heading straight for the bathroom cabinet.*

SUSIE   'Scuse me Mark. Just need to get something. Don't mind do you?

MARK   *(Surprised.)* No, no, go ahead.

SUSIE   Bloody eye liner's gone walk-about again see. Thought I had one in my bag, but when I looked it'd gone, done a Houdini. I'm off out in half an hour and I'm running late. *(Susie finds one.)* Yes! Don't mind if I put it on quickly do you?

MARK   No, not at all.

She begins to apply eye-liner.

SUSIE   Cheers. You're a star. The mirror in my room's knackered. I could do with getting a new one really. Rob reckons I should get one put up over the bed. Says it'd get plenty of use. Cheeky bastard.

MARK   Right.

SUSIE   Where is the old queen anyway? Not still in bed is she?

MARK   Rob? No, he's gone to the shop. We needed some milk.

Susie fishes around in the cupboard and finds a handful of lipsticks.

SUSIE *(Holding out two lipsticks.)* Tropical Orchid or Chiffon Peach?

MARK Sorry?

SUSIE Lipstick? Which one?

MARK What d'you normally wear?

SUSIE Blood of New Born Child.

MARK Peach then.

Susie discards one of the lipsticks and starts to apply the other.

MARK D'you say you were going out?

SUSIE I've got a meeting. That's why I'm going full out with the warpaint. I'm going to see about doing another show.

MARK Great.

SUSIE Nothing's definite. It's just an interview.

MARK Rob said you're very good.

SUSIE Did he? I bet that choked him.

MARK   He was telling me you're working on some new stuff at the moment too. A new routine.

SUSIE   Yeah, that's right. I'm going to start doing Gaynor Hopkins soon. *(Beat)* Bonnie Tyler? Her real name's Gaynor Hopkins? Mind you, Bonnie's not much of an improvement is it? It was Rob's bright spark of an idea. Reckons there'd be plenty of room for a Bonnie Tyler impersonator on a circuit where there aren't any. I've got one or two things to sort out first though before I can crack on. I need a wig. You wouldn't think it but shaggy blonde perms don't come cheap.

Susie crosses over and discovers her trainers beneath a pair of men's jockey shorts. She picks the pair of shorts up and throws it to Mark.

SUSIE   Yours I presume?

MARK   *(Embarrassed.)* Yep, thanks.

SUSIE   Sexy. You'll have to model them for me after.

Susie sits down and pulls on her shoes.

SUSIE   You don't mind me barging in like this do you?

MARK   It's your bathroom.

SUSIE   I've been telling Rob we should get the lock on that door fixed for ages. It's been like that since we moved in.

MARK   You don't mind having it open then?

SUSIE   Not really.   Makes life more exciting doesn't it?   You never know quite what you'll find when you open the door.

Pause.

SUSIE   There's no need to be embarrassed Mark.   I have seen a naked man in the bath before.

MARK   Rob said as much.

SUSIE   Why doesn't that surprise me?

MARK   Could you pass us that towel please?

SUSIE   Had enough have you?

MARK   There's only so much time you can spend in the bath before.....

SUSIE   It shrivels?

MARK   The water gets cold.

Susie holds up the towel while Mark gets out of the bath and wraps himself in it.

MARK   Thanks.

SUSIE   You're welcome.

Mark goes to leave.

SUSIE   Don't drip on that carpet now. Rob goes spare when the carpet gets soaked.

Mark hesitates and decides to stay. Susie goes over to the mirror again and rifles with her hair. Mark reaches for another towel and dries himself, before pulling on a t-shirt.

MARK   Do you want me to have a look at that lock for you then? See if I can fix it?

SUSIE   Could you?

MARK   I could try.

SUSIE   Does that mean you're not planning on going into work today then? No accounting that needs doing?

MARK   No, we're spending the day together.

SUSIE   In for another marathon sex session are you?

MARK   Sorry?

SUSIE   The walls are thin and I'm a light sleeper.

MARK   No, we're going into town. Shopping.

SUSIE   Rob's first love eh? You'll be back later on though won't you?

MARK   I think so. Why?

SUSIE   I think we should go out. The three of us. I haven't seen you both for ages, and I need to catch up with all your news. Besides, I could do with a gin or two.

MARK   I'll see what Rob says.

SUSIE   Good. About eight then? And you never know, I might have something to celebrate too.

MARK   Sorry?

SUSIE   The job? I might get lucky. *(Beat)* I could murder Steve for getting me into this business sometimes.

MARK   Steve?

SUSIE   Well, Rob had a hand in it too. The first time I went up on stage was at his birthday party see. I only did it for a laugh. Slaughtered as usual.

MARK   Rob said you and Steven were good mates.

SUSIE   Yeah well, what can I say? I'm a bad judge of character.

MARK   You don't see him anymore then?

SUSIE   Nope. He's a little shit, and I don't want to have anything to do with him.

MARK   Rob said they were using your bed.

SUSIE   So he's given you all the sordid details? Yes they were in my bed. Caught stark naked, wrapped up together in my duvet, with their tongues in one another's mouths, and they still tried to pretend that nothing was going on. Bastards.

MARK   Rob said it was bad.

SUSIE   Yeah, well, between you and me, the whole thing screwed Rob up for a while. It wrecked him. Well, it would, wouldn't it? You come home from work to find your boyfriend of two years rolling about on your flatmate's bed with another man and it's bound to fuck you up. It has to.

MARK   But you think he's over it now?

SUSIE   Well, he's got you hasn't he? *(Beat)* But I'll tell you one thing for definite Mark. If you shit on him, or if you do anything to screw this up, I'll come looking for you, and by the time I've finished I'll make sure you don't have a chance to do it again alright? I like you Mark. Just don't fuck it up.

Rob appears in the doorway with a pint of milk.

ROB   What's this? Coffee morning?

SUSIE   Nah, we were just swapping beauty tips.

ROB   Didn't think you had any Susie.

SUSIE   People in glass houses Rob.

MARK   Susie was just saying that she'd like for us all to go out tonight.

SUSIE   Quick drink after dinner?

MARK   Sounds all right doesn't it?

ROB   If we're back, yeah.

MARK   Why? What's happening?

ROB   That film. We decided last weekend.

MARK   Oh that thing? Can't we put it off?

ROB   It's the last night. Susie doesn't mind if we go do you?

SUSIE   Me? God no. I'll survive.

ROB   We can go down the pub any time Mark.

SUSIE   Yeah, you two go and enjoy yourselves. It was just an idea. You can snog your way through the credits in the back row. I'll find something else to occupy myself with.

MARK   Are you sure?

SUSIE   Definite. And anyway, I wouldn't want to get in the way of true love and all that now would I? *(Beat)* God, is that the time? I'm going to be so shagging late it's untrue.

Susie heads for the door.

SUSIE   See you later girls. Be good.

Exits.

ROB   And then she was gone.

MARK   Did you have to do that?

ROB   What?

MARK   She really wanted to come out with us tonight.

ROB   Susie doesn't mind.

MARK   She wanted to spend some time with you. It can't be easy for her.

ROB   We'll go out again, tomorrow, it's no big deal. Where's she off to anyway?

MARK   She's gone to see about a job.

ROB *(Approaching Mark.)* So? It's just us two?

MARK   Did you work that one out by yourself?

ROB *(Wrapping his arms around Rob from behind.)* And here you are waiting for me to come home wearing nothing except a damp towel.

MARK   Can't you think about anything else?

ROB *(Kissing Mark's neck.)* No.

MARK   Pathetic.

ROB   We could go into the bedroom?

MARK *(Playfully.)* We just got up.

ROB   Let's stay here then. I don't mind.

MARK   Susie says she can hear us at night.

ROB   Thin walls.

MARK   You knew?

ROB   Don't tell me you haven't heard her snoring?

MARK   You could've said something.

ROB   Like what?

MARK   What're you doing?

ROB   Trying to get your t-shirt off.

MARK   *(Enjoying the play.)* Stop it Rob.

ROB   And then I'm going to get rid of this towel.

MARK   You're obsessed.

ROB   I know. But when I get rid of this towel you'll be naked, and I'll be able stand behind you, feeling every single part of your body.

MARK   Rob.....

ROB   Rubbing my hands all over your chest, your waist, your nipples, the insides of your thighs. I'll be in control and when I want to I'll start to kiss your shoulders, lick your neck, feel your balls, and make you scream because you can't stand it anymore, and then when you're about to come and I'm ready I'll get deep inside you and we'll fuck, just the two of us, here, alone.

Pause. Mark pulls away.

ROB   Hey.

MARK   I thought we were going out this morning.
Rob approaches Mark again.

ROB   We've got all day for that. Come here.

MARK   Not now ok?

ROB   What's wrong?

MARK   Let's just go out eh? I'll get my jeans.

ROB   Mark? Tell me if I've done something wrong.

Pause.

MARK   Do you really want to do that with me?

ROB   What?

MARK   Y'know? That. Is that what you want?

ROB   Well yeah, don't you? I want to get as close to you as I can Mark. We'd use stuff. We'd be safe.

MARK   It's not that. It's just, well, I haven't thought about doing that before.

ROB   Oh, well that's ok. I mean it's not a problem. I just thought..... Sorry. I shouldn't have said anything. *(Beat)* You'd better put some clothes on then if you want to go into town.

Rob exits. Pause before Mark follows.

12. *Inside a stationary car. Luke is sitting in the driver's seat and Susie in the passenger's. They are kissing wildly. The sounds of cars passing can be heard, and their lights occasionally dazzle through the windows. They break away from kissing, and get their breath back before speaking.*

LUKE   Fucking hell.

SUSIE   Yeah.

LUKE   Wow.

SUSIE   Yeah.

LUKE   Jesus.

SUSIE   Yeah.

LUKE   Fuck.

SUSIE   Yeah. *(Beat)* Wanna do it again?

LUKE   Yeah.

They kiss excitedly. Luke tries to slide his hand into Susie's dress. Susie pulls away.

SUSIE   Oi! Not here. I'm not getting them out for you here.

LUKE   Why not?

SUSIE   We're in the middle of the bloody street that's why not.

LUKE   Nobody minds.

SUSIE   Well I do, and I'm not getting my kit off in a parked car in the middle of the street. Not tonight anyway. I haven't had that much to drink.

LUKE   No one's looking.

SUSIE   How do you know?

LUKE   No one's around.

SUSIE   Not now no. But someone might pop along half way through and catch us in full flow.

LUKE   I'm not shy.

SUSIE   I didn't say you were.

Luke sits back and looks out.

LUKE   Can't we go inside?

SUSIE   You're not slow in putting yourself forward are you?

LUKE   I've always been keen. Well?

SUSIE   Maybe.

LUKE   Maybe?

SUSIE   Yeah, maybe, later on. If you behave. There's no rush .
You haven't got a curfew have you?

LUKE   No, but I think it's a bit stupid us sitting round in a cold
car in the middle of the night when there's a nice warm flat lying
empty up there.

SUSIE   It's not empty. My flatmate's in.

LUKE   Is she funny about you bringing blokes home then?

SUSIE   No.

LUKE   Bit up tight is she?

SUSIE   Far from it.

LUKE   Is she the jealous sort then?

SUSIE   Can be. But not at the moment, he's seeing somebody
himself.

LUKE   You share with a bloke? *(Beat)* So he's like a friend
then?

SUSIE   Come again?

LUKE   Well, are you friends or are you like, y'know, special friends?

SUSIE   God no.

LUKE   Gormless is he?

SUSIE   No. Rob is just my friend. That's all. Nothing else. We've never shared any bodily fluids whatsoever, just a toilet seat.

LUKE   So he's up there now then?

SUSIE   Yep.

LUKE   With his woman?

SUSIE   Sort of.

LUKE   Sort of?

SUSIE   He's up there with his boyfriend.

LUKE   Oh God, right, I'm with you now. He's gay.

SUSIE   Yes.

LUKE   And he's up there with his bloke? On the job like?

SUSIE   Probably.

LUKE   So why don't you want to go upstairs then? Don't want to disturb them is it?

SUSIE   He's got his own room.

LUKE   So what's the problem?

SUSIE   I just want to stay here for a bit. Admire the view. If that's ok with you?

Pause. Luke looks out the window bemused.

LUKE   So, you don't mind it then? You're not trying to stay out of their way because you don't like it? Them? At it?

SUSIE   No. They can bonk away till the end of the millennium for all I care. I'll even cheer them on. I just don't want to go in right now. I want to sit here. With you.

LUKE   Fine. You're the boss. D'you want the radio on?

SUSIE   Nah.

Pause.

LUKE   The blower?

SUSIE   Thanks, but I'm right.

Pause. He produces a tin of travel sweets.

LUKE   Butterscotch?

SUSIE   Look I'm fine. I don't want anything. So can we just sit here for a minute please? Quietly? There's nothing suspicious about it. I just want to sit here, in your nice new Metro for five minutes before going back into that flat and getting you to give me the screw of the century on the bedroom carpet. All right? Ok?

LUKE   Fine.

SUSIE   Thank you.

Pause.

LUKE   *(Timidly.)* It's a Peugeot though. Not a Metro. I'd never buy a Metro. My Dad had one once but the suspension went and.....

SUSIE   It just pisses me off that's all. He farts around for nine months because his boyfriend leaves him, pours his heart out to me, refuses to go anywhere, feels sorry for himself, and I do my best, I try to cheer him up, take his mind off it, and what happens? Bang! He meets this man, nice man, I've got nothing against this man, he's fine, lovely, polite, clean, but they're suddenly in love, and everything's hunky-dory hokey-cokey all over again. It's like the last sodding nine months never happened. And where does that leave me? Sitting in front of the bloody tv, while they go out to dinner together, and spend every waking second of the day together, that's where. But it's not on is it? It's not fair?

LUKE   No.

SUSIE   And now what's happened? They've fallen so much in love that they've decided to move in together. To move in to my flat. They've even started buying Le Crueset kitchen ware for the love nest. And what about me? What if I don't want to be stuck in the middle, playing sodding Happy Families? What then? What happens if I actually turn round and say to the two of them, 'Excuse me lads, but I live here too you know, and I want a bit of consideration. I pay half the rent, I laid out good money for that bed settee you keep raping each other on, and I don't particularly want to see you making eyes at each other over the breakfast table anymore.' What happens then eh?

Luke shrugs his shoulders.

SUSIE   They get pissed off don't they? They start making funny comments. Start giving me funny looks. Start putting name tags on the milk and the bread. 'This pint of milk is Rob and Mark's'. 'This loaf belongs to us, not you Susie. So bugger off and buy your own.' That's what'll happen. And I don't want that. I just want them to consider my feelings every so often. I just want them, once in a while, to say, 'Ah, Susie, fancy coming down the pub for a quick beer mate?' or, 'Wanna share a pizza Susie?', or even, 'Hey Susie, d'you mind if we lounge around on your sofa nibbling each other's toe nails for the next half hour while you try and watch the telly.' Is that too much? Is that going too far?

LUKE   No.

SUSIE   Thank you.

Pause.

LUKE   Do they really nibble each other's toe nails?

SUSIE   And spit out the remains in the ashtray? Yes, they do.

LUKE   You should say something.

SUSIE   I wouldn't know what to say.

LUKE   I think you would.

SUSIE   Maybe.

LUKE   Do it. Walk up to them and tell them you're pissed off.

SUSIE   You reckon?

LUKE   For definite.

SUSIE   Ok. I'll say something.

LUKE   Good.

SUSIE   I'll be subtle.

LUKE   Good.

SUSIE   But direct.

Pause.

SUSIE   Don't suppose you fancy coming in for a cup of tea do you?

LUKE   I was starting to think you'd never ask.

13. *Bathroom. Night. Mark is using a screwdriver to fit the new lock to the door. Rob watches.*

MARK   Are you sure she doesn't mind then?

ROB   Look, she'd say if she didn't want you round the place.

MARK   D'you reckon?

ROB   Believe me, she'd have made it perfectly clear by now if she didn't want you moving in. She'd have told you to your face. Ask her yourself if you don't believe me.

MARK   Ok. I will. Where is she tonight anyway?

ROB   Some nasty old club one of her friends likes. She won't be back for hours yet. *(Beat)* I still can't believe you're actually going to fix that door. It's been broken for ages.

MARK   All the more reason to repair it then.

ROB   Didn't know you were so handy.

MARK   There's nothing to it, and it needed fixing.

ROB   We've managed without it for long enough.

MARK   Well you won't have to anymore then will you? Doesn't it ever piss you off that you can't just lock the door and have a bath without worrying whether or not someone's going to barge in?

ROB   There's no secrets in this house.

MARK   Or privacy.

ROB   Steven would've liked it. He hated not having a lock on the door. He wouldn't go to the toilet unless he'd made sure that everyone in the flat knew he was going to be in here and promised hand on heart not to walk in. He was always worrying that someone was going to interrupt him half way through. Strange boy.

MARK   You don't miss him then?

ROB   You are joking aren't you? *(No response)* Aren't you?

MARK   Yes. I'm joking.

ROB   No. I don't miss him. I've got other things to keep me occupied now. I'm with you. You. So get used to it yeah?

MARK   Sorry.

Mark kisses Rob.

ROB   So you should be. Besides, Steven couldn't have just done that. He could never have fixed that lock.

MARK   It was nothing.

ROB   Does it work?

MARK   Yes. 'Course it does.

Rob slides the lock shut.

MARK   Well?

ROB   Fantastic.

MARK   Arse.

ROB   Flattery eh?

MARK   Yeah. I've been told it'll get me everywhere.

ROB   *(Holding Mark.)*   God, I love you. I love you so fucking much. You know that don't you? You know that I love you?

MARK   Really?

ROB   Really.

MARK   We're in deep aren't we?

ROB   Over our heads.

MARK   Rob. You won't hurt me will you?

ROB   What?

MARK   If we did it. You wouldn't hurt me? I want to let you. I mean, I want to try. I'm ready to try it, with you.

ROB   Mark....

MARK   Rob. I want to. With you. I want to let you do it.

ROB   Are you sure?

MARK   This is it isn't it?

ROB   You really want to try?

MARK   With you. With you.

They look at one another and then move in to kiss each other very, very slowly.

14. *Kitchen. Morning. Luke drinks from a milk carton just as Rob enters.*

ROB   D'you want a glass for that?

Pause.

ROB   You here with Susie?

LUKE   Yeah, I stayed over.

ROB   D'you have a good time last night then?

LUKE   Not bad. Susie's one hell of a girl. I couldn't keep up with her half the time.

ROB   You off home?

LUKE   To work, yeah. They'll have my balls on a plate if I don't show my face today.

ROB   Susie still in bed?

LUKE   Dead to the world. Didn't want to disturb her. We didn't get much sleep last night. *(Beat)* I'm not doing a runner or anything. I've left my number. She's a nice girl. *(Pause)* Will you tell her I had to get off then? It's a pisser I've got to go at all but I'll have to get home, get in the shower, and change before heading in. And I bet there's no hot water.

ROB   Sure.

LUKE Right then.

ROB   Right.

LUKE I'll probably see you next week. When Susie does her show?

ROB   Show?

LUKE Yeah, y'know? Her big Bonnie Tyler gig? Sounds like a riot. Is your bloke going to be there?

ROB   Sorry?

LUKE Mark is it? Susie said you were seeing someone.

ROB   She did?

LUKE Reckons it's serious. Says he's a nice guy and everything like. Gone has he?

ROB   To work? Yeah.

LUKE So he'll be coming then?

ROB   To the show? Probably. He hasn't seen Susie in action yet either.

LUKE   We'll have something in common then?

ROB   Yeah, see you there.

LUKE   Definitely.   It'll be a laugh.   Anyway, I'd better be making tracks.   Say hi to Sus' for me yeah?   Nice to meet you.   By the way - I'm Luke.

Awkwardly they shake hands.

ROB   Rob.

Luke exits.   Rob picks up the milk carton and throws it away. He moves around the room.   Steven appears in the doorway. Rob senses someone's presence.

ROB   D'you forget something?

Rob turns to face the door.

ROB   Steven.

STEVEN   I was coming up the stairs and some guy was leaving. The door was open.   You don't mind do you?   He said someone was here.

ROB   He was here with Susie.   The guy on the way out.

STEVEN   Right.   Another conquest?   Some things don't change do they?   *(Beat)* How are you?

ROB   Fine.

STEVEN   And Susie?

ROB   Her usual self, y'know?

STEVEN   I'd better keep a low profile then. Is she still doing the cabaret?

ROB   Just about.

STEVEN   Same as ever?

ROB   She's doing a new character now.

STEVEN   Yeah? Who?

ROB   Bonnie Tyler.

STEVEN   Excellent.

ROB   It is.

STEVEN   Your idea?

ROB   How d'you guess?

STEVEN   Sounds like you. And you're still at the record shop? I mean, I've seen you in there a couple of times. Didn't want to come up and say hi. Well, I did, but I wasn't sure if it'd be welcome. *(Beat)* The flat hasn't changed much. Still just the two of you living here?

ROB   Er, no.

STEVEN   Oh, has someone else moved in? The guy making the quick exit?

ROB   No. Mark lives here now. Mark. With me.

STEVEN   Oh. Right.

ROB   Are you still seeing Gareth?

STEVEN   We finished a few months back.

ROB   Sorry.

STEVEN   No you're not. *(Beat)* I'm glad I caught you Rob. I wasn't sure if you were working. I wanted to come round. I wanted to see how you were. It's been a while hasn't it? Eighteen months must be.

ROB   Is it? Feels like longer to be honest.

STEVEN   Yeah well, I don't blame you for being pissed off with me Rob. I did behave like a total wanker.

ROB   Won't argue with you there.

STEVEN   And I still don't know why I did it.   It still doesn't make sense, if that means anything to you.

ROB   Like you said, it's been a long time.   A lot's happened.

STEVEN   Obviously.

ROB   Sorry?

STEVEN   Well it hasn't taken you very long to find someone else has it?

ROB   I don't know Steve, eighteen months seems like plenty of time to me.

STEVEN   Is he here today then?   This Mark?

ROB   Look Steve.   What d'you want?   Why've you come round?

STEVEN   I wanted to see you.

ROB   After all this time?

STEVEN   I thought I should come round. I've been thinking about you a lot lately, and well, I wanted to come over.

ROB   What? Don't tell me you've actually come round to apologize?

STEVEN   Don't make this any harder for me Rob please.

ROB   Harder? It hasn't been a walkover for me either you know? Ok, so it's been eighteen months but I still don't understand how you could've done that. How you could hurt me like that?

STEVEN   Coming round seemed like a good idea last night. Something I had to do.

ROB   Why Steve? What were you thinking about?

STEVEN   I'm sorry if you're still upset but I had to come over because I've got something I need to tell you.

ROB   You were naked.

STEVEN   I've been practising the words for weeks now and I still can't say it.

ROB   Kissing him. Loving him. And then you saw me. You looked sideways and you saw me standing there.

STEVEN   This isn't easy Rob.

ROB   I had to find you together, and when I did, all you could do was smile at me. I was staring at you both in bed and all you could do was grin back at me.

STEVEN   I've been to see someone.....

ROB   I could feel my insides tightening. I thought my heart was going to crack.....

STEVEN   They did some tests.....

ROB   And just as I'm getting over you, just as I'm sorting my life out you decide to come round because you need to talk to me. So what's so important Steve? What's brought you back? What's the problem?

STEVEN   I'm positive. HIV positive.

15. *Bonnie Tyler's 'Total Eclipse of the Heart' plays. The lights rise on Susie dressed as Bonnie Tyler. She is in the complete outfit, wig, and make-up. She steps forward with a microphone as though on stage and performs to the song; miming enthusiastically. The music fades towards the end and the sound of the sea crashing against the shore is heard again.*

16. *Lights rise on Rob standing alone. The sounds of the sea crashing against the shore continue.*

ROB   If the balance is lost, if too much weight falls on any one side of the raft, then you could be in trouble. If the raft loses its balance then you could fall, you could drop into the water. And if you should fall, you may never be able to climb back up on to the raft again.

Fade.

Act Two

1. *Lights rise to reveal Susie standing alone. She is dressed in one of her stage outfits. The lighting suggests that she might actually be on stage.*

SUSIE   The first time it happened it was funny. Not hysterical, roll about on your arse funny, but amusing. Well it is now. When I look back at it.

Exactly one month older than me, David was tall, blonde, rugged, and far too gorgeous to be mine. I should have known there was a snag, I should have known it wasn't going to last, and I should have known he was queer when he asked me back to his house to play his new Pet Shop Boys record. But I didn't. And while we sat on his bed, listening to 'It's A Sin', eating Maltesers, and reading the problem pages, I fell for him, with a crash.

It wasn't until one of my best mates pointed out that it was quite unusual for a boy David's age to have a giant poster of Jason Donovan above his bed, and an Erasure Tour of Europe t-shirt hanging in his wardrobe, that I started to question the exact nature of our relationship. And when I confronted him he admitted that yes, he didn't feel as strongly about girls as the other boys in school seemed to, and confessed that yes, like me, he was inexplicably attracted to Henry Ramsey out of *Neighbours*.

Getting over David didn't take long. A quick snog from Paul Morgans at the next school disco saw to that. But Paul Morgans didn't equal love, not proper make-your-heart-go-boom love, and it wasn't until I met Steven that I thought I could ever be sucked in like that again. I pursued Steven like a woman possessed. I left notes for him inside his lever-arch file, and wrote 'I love you' on his pencil case with Tipp-Ex. But however much I worshipped him it didn't seem to get me anywhere nearer a snog, and it wasn't until we'd left school and he'd gone off to college that I found out why. He was gay. Strike two. I seemed to be getting good at weeding them out, and could probably have landed myself a successful career with the military police.

Standing tall, back on my feet, with a new improved smile, Steven and I remained friends. We still saw each other, enjoyed indulgent evenings together, sitting in front of the tv awarding the latest soap stud marks out of ten for body shape, beauty, and most importantly, shagability. The perfect match. We'd go to clubs together and spend the night sussing out possible partners for one another, and it was during such a night out that I spotted Rob across the dancefloor. Beautiful Rob. He was mine, I knew he had to be mine.

But by the end of the night, as I left empty-handed, I realized that it wasn't going to happen. Rob and Steve were swapping telephone numbers and tongues in the car park. Strike three.

Sounds of waves against the shore crash in and continue as the lights fade.

2. *Bathroom. Night. Luke is sitting on the toilet seat and Susie is sitting on his lap. They are kissing. Luke tries to push his hand into Susie's top.*

SUSIE   Oi.

LUKE   What?

SUSIE   Paws off. Mark's in.

LUKE   So?

SUSIE   Well, what's he going to say if we start doing it here and now on the bathroom floor?

LUKE   We haven't got to tell him have we?

SUSIE   You know what I mean.

Susie gets up and goes to the bathroom cabinet. She starts to put on some lipstick.

SUSIE   Besides, it'll do you good to wait. You've been getting your own way far too often lately.

LUKE   I haven't heard you complaining.

Luke moves in behind Susie, and starts kissing the back of her neck.

SUSIE   Luke.

LUKE   It's all about spontaneity.

SUSIE   What is?

LUKE   A healthy sex-life. I read it in one of your girly mags. I'm only trying to be the sensitive and loving partner you want me to be.

SUSIE   Is that right?

LUKE   Aha.

SUSIE   What else did it say then?

LUKE   *(Still kissing her.)* It said that we should make love whenever we want to, as often as we can, and in as many new and exciting situations as we can find.

SUSIE   You'll have me dressing up in rubber next.

LUKE   Is that an offer? You could always slip into your Bonnie Tyler outfit and pull on a pair of crotchless knickers. I've always wanted to do it with an international super star.

SUSIE   Not funny.

LUKE   Or maybe you've got one or two friends that might like to come over and play a few games.

SUSIE   You're mental.

LUKE   You've noticed?

SUSIE   Kinked.

LUKE   Oh, I'll try anything once. Twice if I like it.

SUSIE   Get off.

LUKE   Yes Miss. Sorry Miss. I love it when you tell me off Miss.

SUSIE   Can't you control yourself for five minutes?

LUKE   Why? What happens in five minutes?

SUSIE   Mark'll go to bed.

LUKE   And then?

SUSIE   Then I'll show you a little technique I learnt for myself in one of those magazines you haven't been reading.

LUKE   Can't wait.

SUSIE   Well you'll just have to.

LUKE   Tease.

SUSIE   I've been called worse.

LUKE   I thought they were going out tonight anyway? I thought they were going to make themselves scarce so that we could have a bit of privacy.

SUSIE   They were. Until Rob didn't come home.

LUKE   Problems at work?

SUSIE   Don't know. He was supposed to be back by six but hasn't turned up.

LUKE   Hasn't he phoned?

Susie shakes her head.

LUKE   God, I bet Mark's pissed off.

SUSIE   He's been behaving like a complete wanker all week. Staying out late. Sniping at everyone. Treating Mark like shit.

LUKE   So what's up?

SUSIE   Wish I knew. Mark thinks he's going off him.

LUKE   And is he?

SUSIE   I've given up trying to work out what goes on inside that boy's head. We used to be so tight once that I doubt I could've carried on without him. But now... Now I can hardly find anything to say to him, and he hasn't got anything to say to me, so, we don't bother.

LUKE   Pity. You've been friends ages.

SUSIE   Yeah, well. I've got you now haven't I?

LUKE   You certainly have.

SUSIE   Sounds serious.

LUKE   Does it? Perhaps it was supposed to. Well, this is more than just a fling isn't it? I mean, tell me if I'm wrong, but there's a lot more going on here isn't there Susie?

SUSIE   Yeah. I suppose. *(Beat)* No, definitely. If you say so.

LUKE   I'm not trying to push you. I'm not trying to scare you off, but, but I don't think I've ever felt like this before. No pressure of course.

SUSIE   Of course. No pressure.

They kiss. Susie begins to unbuckle Luke's belt.

LUKE   Hey, what's going on down below?

SUSIE   I'm about to take your trousers off. Have you got a problem with that?

LUKE   No, no. Carry on. But what about Mark?

SUSIE   He can take his own trousers off.

They continue playing around. Luke pulls away briefly.

LUKE   Susie?

SUSIE   What? You're not chickening out are you?

LUKE   Condoms. They're in the bedroom.

SUSIE   Luke!

LUKE   I'll just pop out and get them. Hold it right there.

SUSIE   No, no, stay, don't worry about it.

LUKE   But.....

SUSIE   It'll spoil the moment.

LUKE   What about.....

SUSIE   Just shut up Luke. It's ok. I've got it covered.

LUKE   It's lucky you've got a lock on that door.

Sound of waves against the shore start up and continue into the next scene.

3. *Evening. A beach. It is beginning to get dark.*

ROB   When did you find out?

STEVEN   Few months back. Some of the guys at work were going into town to give blood at lunch-time, so I went along. I got a letter back a few weeks later to tell me that they couldn't use my blood.

ROB   And they're sure?

STEVEN   Yeah.

ROB   Jesus.

STEVEN   It feels like I've been in a daze for ages. Trying to get my head round it. Trying to suss it out. I'm glad you phoned.

ROB   It was a shock that's all.

STEVEN   Sorry. But I had to come over. I needed to talk. You don't mind do you?

ROB   You're just lucky Susie was tucked up in bed.

STEVEN   Have you told her?

ROB   Nah. She's too wrapped up with Luke to be bothered about anything else at the moment.

STEVEN   Luke?

ROB   Mr.Right. They're inseparable.

STEVEN   You do understand why I called in though don't you?

ROB   Is this why Gareth left?

STEVEN   He couldn't handle it.

ROB   Has he tested?

STEVEN   Don't know. He won't return my calls, won't even come to the door if I go round to see him.

ROB   Do you think that I've got it then? Is that why you came to see me?

STEVEN   No Rob. I just came round to tell you. To let you know.

ROB   But I could have it?

STEVEN   I don't know. It's possible.

ROB   But if you've only just found out it's unlikely isn't it? I mean we haven't slept together for well over a year. Ages really.

STEVEN   I've only just been diagnosed Rob. I could've been infected a long time ago. It might've been recently, before we met, or it could've been when we were together.

ROB   You mean, I gave it to you?

STEVEN   You don't even know what your HIV status is yet.

ROB   But if you got it when you were with me, then I must have passed it on to you. Who else could it have been?

STEVEN   Rob.....

ROB   There wasn't anyone else was there? Was there?

STEVEN   A bit of fun, that's all, a laugh. Nothing serious.

ROB   For fuck's sake Steve.

STEVEN   They didn't mean anything.

ROB   No? So why did you go with them then?

Pause.

ROB   I can't believe, I can't believe you could do that. Not when I was so honest with you.

STEVEN   It was once or twice. I can't explain why it happened.

ROB   So that means you might have got it from someone else then? You might not have had it from me after all?

STEVEN   It doesn't matter who infected me Rob.

ROB   But if it wasn't me, then I'm clear. I don't have to worry.

STEVEN   We were together for a long time though.

ROB   And we were safe. We looked after ourselves.

STEVEN   Did we?

ROB   I can't stand this. Last week I'm on top form. Everything's coming together at last, and now, and now I can't even sleep at night because I'm so frightened that I've got this shit running about inside of me. Jesus Steve, why did you have to come round? Why did you have to tell me?

STEVEN   You'll have to get it sorted Rob. You'll have to find out for sure. You can't carry on speculating like this.

ROB   Why not?

STEVEN   It's best to know. So you can take steps.

ROB   But chances are there's nothing wrong with me. I mean, I'd know if there was something to worry about. I'd feel it wouldn't I?

STEVEN   If you tested you'd know.

ROB   But if I was positive then I really wouldn't want to know.

I'd rather carry on living without having to face that, without worrying. I couldn't hack knowing. I'd want to die if I ever found out.

Pause.

ROB   Ste.....

STEVEN   No. You're right. You do want to die. You do want to end it all right there and then. You don't want this bastard virus running around inside you, fucking you up, breaking you down so that every time you cough or sneeze you panic. You don't want to be scared. But if you test, you can get a grip on things. It's just a test Rob. It could always come up negative.

ROB   Exactly. A test isn't going to tell me anything I don't already know, and if I'm not ill then it isn't a problem, is it?

STEVEN   You'll never hide from it Rob. You've got to get on top of it.

ROB   Thanks Steve, but don't worry about it eh? It's under control.

Sound of waves against the shore continue as the lights fade.

4. Bathroom. Night. The room is in darkness. Rob is standing by the sink, he switches on the light and looks into the mirror. Mark appears in the doorway a moment later.

MARK   You all right?

ROB   Yeah. Tremendous thanks.

Mark comes in and switches on another light. He closes the door behind him.

MARK   I heard you come in. You've been out a long time.

ROB   We went for a drink after work.

MARK   But you've been out all night?

ROB   Don't you believe me?

MARK   Yeah. 'Course. If you say that's where you were, then fine, I believe you.

ROB   No you don't. You don't believe a word I say anymore, and you're not very good at pretending. So don't bother eh? It's painful.

MARK   I was worried. I thought something might have happened.

ROB   Well, sorry to disappoint you Marky, but I'm back, in one piece, safe and sound.

MARK   You coming to bed then?

No reply.

MARK   D'you want me to get you something?

ROB   Yeah, you can stop fannying around. For fuck's sake Mark, you don't let up do you?

MARK   I was only.....

ROB   Well don't. Don't do anything. Just go back to bed, bury your head under the pillow, enjoy your sweet little wet dreams, and leave me alone eh? Just leave me.

MARK   Rob? What's going on?

ROB   Nothing.

MARK   Come off it.....

ROB   Nothing's going on. I just want to be left alone. I'm just a sad bastard trying to enjoy his own company for once. You should try it some time.

MARK   Nothing?

ROB   Nothing.

MARK   So why have you been avoiding me then?

ROB   I haven't. I can't.

MARK   There you go again. Sticking the knife in every chance you get. So what's the problem?

ROB   I haven't got a problem.

MARK   Why didn't you come home? I was waiting for you. I was ready to go out.

ROB   You should have gone.

MARK   We agreed to go together.

ROB   You don't need me to hold your hand.

MARK   See what I mean? You can't resist taking a shot can you?

ROB   You're an easy target.

MARK   For God's sake Rob. I'm doing my best here. I'm trying to get some sense out of you. Look, if this is your way of telling me that it's over then I'd rather you just told me ok? Just tell me and get it over with.

No reply.

MARK   You're impossible.

ROB   Yeah. That's right. Me. Impossible. It's always the way isn't it? I'm always the one that's done wrong. Well, not everyone can live up to your high standards Mark, not everyone's quite so perfect as you, and perhaps if you took five minutes out of your busy, but I'm sure well organized schedule to realise that, then you might just begin to understand me. You might understand that I'm not the problem.

MARK   How much have you had to drink?

ROB   Not enough probably. But I like it. It makes me happy. It turns me on.

MARK   It's about the only thing that does then.

ROB   Wa-hey! Now who's being a little bitch?

MARK   Sort it out Rob. You're beyond a joke.

ROB   You're so sodding uptight aren't you? So righteous. So fucking proper. It's sad really. You're so busy running your own little organised life that you just can't give in for five seconds can you? Can't kick back. Don't know how to let go.

MARK   I'm going to bed.

ROB   At last.

MARK   I don't have to listen to this Rob. I don't have to stand here and listen to your shit.

ROB   Why do you then?

MARK   I don't know. But I don't have to.

ROB   Yeah, right. Like you've got a choice? And what exactly would you be doing with yourself if you weren't here with me tonight then Marky? Propping up a bar somewhere? Touring the toilets? Hoping that someone'd feel sorry for you, take you home with them, let you climb into their bed? Just like the good old days eh?

MARK   You bastard.

ROB   Getting angry are we? God, that must be a new emotion for you.

MARK   How can you.....

ROB   But after all that, after all that effort, the really funny thing is that you didn't even know what to do when you did get yourself into someone else's bed. Didn't even know how to kiss properly. You just lay there, motionless. Waiting for something to happen, for me to touch you, for me to make a move. Waiting for me to get on top of you, hold you, show you what you were missing out on. I even had to bloody undress you you were so nervous. So don't pretend that you could just walk away from me Mark, because I know different.

The door swings open. Luke appears. Susie is standing behind. They are only partly dressed.

LUKE   Everything all right guys?

ROB   Ah here they come. Terry and June.

MARK   Yes thanks. Go back to bed. We're fine.

LUKE   You sure?

MARK   Yeah. It's ok.

ROB   Go on, piss off back to bed. You've been shagging away like monkeys all week, so why stop now just because we're making a bit of noise for a change?

SUSIE Stop it Rob.

ROB   I was wondering how long it'd take you to close your legs and open your gob.

SUSIE   Shut it.

ROB   When I want your advice I'll ask for it, ok?

SUSIE   You're so fucking up your own arse it's untrue.

ROB   Oh, go back to your soiled sheets Susie. Stick to what you know best eh? Get super dick here to give you a good seeing to.

LUKE   Oi! Apologize.

ROB   Well that's what you want isn't it? You want Susie to give you some? She's always giving some. Very generous. Very good by all accounts.

LUKE   You're way out of line Rob.

ROB   Yeah? Well, what're you going to do about it? Smack me?

SUSIE   Leave him Luke. He's pissed.

LUKE   That's no excuse. He's got no right to talk to you like that.

SUSIE   Leave it. He's not worth it.

MARK   Luke. I'll see to it.

LUKE   You haven't got to take this Mark.

MARK   It'll be fine.

LUKE   You shouldn't let him get away with it. It's pathetic.

MARK   Just give me five minutes eh?

Luke and Susie leave.

ROB   See ya!

Mark shuts the door. Pause. Mark goes over to Rob. Things are calmer now.

MARK   What's going on inside your head Rob? You're frightening me.

ROB   You don't know what it means to be frightened.

MARK   What's happened Rob? What's been going on?

ROB   You don't want to know.

MARK   Talk to me Rob. Tell me.

ROB   How can everything go from being so fucking brilliant to this eh?

MARK   What's happened?

ROB   You really want me to tell you? You honestly want to know? I had a visitor. Here at the flat. Steven. Yeah, blast from the past or what eh? He came over last week. He came over to tell me. To tell me that he's tested HIV positive. Pisser eh? *(Pause)* But, that's it. That's what's wrong. Happy now? Happy that you finally know exactly what's been screwing me up?

Pause.

MARK   Is he sure?

ROB   'Course he is.

MARK   When did he find out?

ROB   He went to give blood.

MARK   But you're not supposed to give..... Have you been down to test?

ROB   No.

MARK   But if he was HIV positive when you were together then he might have passed it on.....

ROB   We were safe.

MARK   For two whole years? How can you be sure?

ROB   I just am ok?

MARK   But if you're HIV positive then I..... Oh, for fuck's sake Rob. For fuck's sake.

ROB   Mark.

MARK   But we've done everything together. I let you.....

ROB   We used a condom.....

MARK   For fuck's sake.....

ROB   You're all right.

MARK   Am I?

ROB   Yes. We looked out for each other.

MARK   What? Like Steven did, you mean?

ROB   This is different.

MARK   How?

ROB   It just is.

MARK   We'll have to test. We'll have to go down and test.

ROB   No.

MARK   We can go tomorrow. Get it done.

ROB   I'm not testing Mark.

MARK   You'll have to find out. They'll do a blood test. They'll tell us within days, and then we'll know where we stand and we can sort it out. We'll go to the clinic tomorrow yeah? Rob?

ROB   I can't.

MARK   You have to.

ROB   Didn't you hear me? I don't want to know.

MARK   You can't pretend he never told you. That it hasn't been said.

ROB   Listen to me. I can't. I can't walk down there, I can't go in and ask for the test, I can't sit there while they take the blood, and I can't watch some doctor squaring up to give me my result. I'm scared. Scared ok? Scared that I'll be positive.

MARK   But that's why you've got to go. That's why you've got to find out. Think about it at least.

ROB   *(Breaking down towards the end.)* Think about it? Think? Mark, I can't stop thinking about it. I can't stop churning it around inside my head, thinking about it. That's the trouble. If only I could forget about it. Forget that it was ever a possibility. Forget that I might have it. Forget that I've got to keep thinking about it. Every second of the day, it's there, and when it's getting to me, smothering me, I decide, 'Right, get tested Rob, find out exactly what the situation is.' And that's when I start getting frightened. Frightened because I don't want to be positive, and all it'd mean. And that's when I remember the nights when I wasn't that sensible, nights when it didn't seem to matter, when it felt like I was going to live forever. Nights when I really felt alive, nights when I was really living. And that's why I know I can't do it. I know. I can't face it. I can't.....

MARK *(Holding him.)* Sssh. Sssh. Rob. We'll sort it out. We'll sort it.

The sound of the waves crashing against the shore swells up again.

5. Lights up on Luke standing alone.

LUKE   Dating was so much easier when you were thirteen, zit ridden, and obsessed with breasts. There were no rules then. No standards to live up to. Boys and girls were divided by a stretch of tarmac playground, where they could eye one another up suspiciously from a safe distance. The problems only started when your best mates developed hormones and talked you into crossing that no-man's land towards the huddle of giggling girls on the other side, who were lost in the pages of *Smash Hits*, and you'd have to ask one of them, usually the one ear marked by your mates as the best of the bunch, and say, without fear of rejection, 'D'you wanna go with me then?' And after the giggling had died down the girl would pluck the ball of chewing gum from her mouth and say, 'Yeah. S'pose.' And from there on you'd be in a relationship, you'd be in love, you'd be going together.

Going together was a funny kind of relationship that didn't mean commitment or sex. It was a relationship that involved being seen together holding hands in the bus bay, comparing homework, and wandering aimlessly around the shopping centre on Saturday afternoons when all you really wanted to do was stay home and watch the footie. No love. No romance. No messing. Just a bit of an occasional fumble and a badly executed snog.

6. *Kitchen. Evening. Luke is smoking a cigarette. There is an opened bottle of wine on the table. Mark enters.*

MARK   I thought there was someone in here.

Luke offers Mark a cigarette. He declines.

LUKE   Yeah, I'm going to give them up one day too. Tomorrow maybe.

MARK   Is that yours?

LUKE   Aha. Help yourself.

Mark picks up the bottle and pours a glass.

MARK   Ta.

LUKE   Where's Rob?

MARK   He's gone down to see Susie. To apologize.

LUKE   Yeah well, he didn't make any new friends last night did he?

MARK   Sorry. He was upset.

LUKE   Upset? It sounded like he was ready to kill you.

MARK   He needed to let rip. Sorry.

LUKE   Yeah, well, as long as he doesn't make a habit of it. Susie said she'd never seen him so manic.

MARK   He knows he was out of order. That's why he's made the effort tonight. He wanted to make it up to her.

LUKE   And what about you? Are you ok?

Mark shrugs.

LUKE   I don't know how you do it mate. After all that shit he gave you last night I'm surprised you didn't walk. If anyone'd given me a mouthful like that I'd be long gone by now.

MARK   That's the problem isn't it? I can't. I love him too much.

Luke takes the bottle back and refills his glass.

MARK   This is nice.

LUKE   Not bad is it? My ex got given a crate of the stuff last Christmas.

MARK   Expensive?

LUKE   I hope so. She dropped me for some skinny bastard with glasses.

Luke offers the bottle to Mark again. He takes it and drinks.

171

LUKE   I'll give you one thing though.   You've got a lot more patience than I have. I wouldn't have been so understanding.

MARK   Yeah well, some people wouldn't call it patience. They'd say I was just stupid.

LUKE   And are you?

MARK   No. Maybe. Oh, I don't know. I don't want to think about it. I'm too tired. All I know is that I can't just give up. For some stupid fucking reason I can't explain, I love him, you know? And I can't give up. To be totally honest he's the only guy I've ever really felt anything for. The only guy I've ever been out with. *(Beat)* God that's sad.

LUKE   Why?

MARK   Well, everyone's got a history haven't they? Everyone's got a first boyfriend, second boyfriend, good shag, bad shag? Everyone fools around before getting involved don't they? Apart from me that is.

LUKE   I'm surprised. I'd have thought a good-looking bloke like you would have had a fair few offers along the way. Jesus, when I think of all the women I've been out with..... He's the only one?

MARK   He's got such a hold over me, it's unreal. I'm even feeling guilty for talking about him now, even after how he behaved last night. Right now I'm thinking I should be having this conversation with him, not someone I've only known, what, a fortnight?

LUKE   You're going to hang on in there then?

MARK   I want to. I've got to try and sort it out.

The bottle passes back to Mark.

MARK   What about you and Susie? How's that going?

LUKE   Early days mate.

MARK   She seems really happy.

LUKE   Yeah, I mean, it's good. Don't get me wrong, I like her. I'm just not sure whether it'll last that's all.

MARK   Another chapter in your search to find the ideal woman eh?

LUKE   Sounds desperate doesn't it?

MARK   Not at all. I wish I was as sorted as you.

LUKE   I wouldn't call myself sorted.

MARK   Compared to me you are. You've got everything under control. You know exactly what you're doing and I like that. I like it that you're not prepared to take second best.

LUKE   It's just my big guy act kicking in. Deep down I don't think I really know what I want or who I want.

MARK   Don't worry. You'll find someone at the end of it all.

LUKE   God, now you sound like my mother. 'You'll find her. You'll pick a nice one. When you least expect it you'll find her. She's waiting for you somewhere.'

MARK   But isn't that what everyone wants? Isn't everyone hoping that at the end of the day they're going to find someone they can call theirs? Someone to make up a pair, someone that's in it forever? That'll balance everything out? Who knows? You and Susie might go the distance.

LUKE   I don't know.

MARK   So why haven't you moved on to the next one?

LUKE   Like you. Maybe I'm frightened. After all, I've got to run out of lives one day haven't I? There's got to be a limit. A point when the game's over and I've got to stop pissing around.

MARK   *(Starting to break down.)* I just wish everything wasn't so difficult y'know? I wish last night hadn't happened. I wish....

LUKE   *(Putting a hand on his shoulder to comfort him.)* Hey mate, come on now. Don't get upset eh? It's not worth it.

MARK   All I've ever wanted is to find someone and be happy.

And now when I've got it, when I thought I had it all, it's about to fall apart.

LUKE   Mark? Mate? Don't do this to me please. Don't get upset.

MARK   I don't want to be on my own again Luke. I couldn't face that.

LUKE   Hey, hey, pal. Don't get upset. Please. Don't cry mate. Don't cry.

MARK   Sorry.

LUKE   I'm just not very good with tears mate. I never know what to do when someone's starts blubbing on me.

MARK   *(Starting to cry again.)* I can't lose him Luke. I can't.

LUKE   Oh Mark. Don't let him upset you. Rob's not worth all this. He really isn't mun. Please mate. Please stop.

Luke still has his hand cupped around Mark's neck.

LUKE   Mark? Please?

Awkward pause. Luke kisses him to make it better. They look at each other.

LUKE   All right?

They kiss again. Difficult pause. Mark pulls back.

7. *Susie is getting ready to go on stage in her dressing room. She is putting on make-up using a table mirror. Rob stands behind her. The crowd and the music from the club outside is heard distantly.*

ROB   Nervous?

SUSIE   *(Noticing him for the first time.)*   You're not about to throw another mental are you? You're not going to lose it on me here are you?

ROB   Sorry.

SUSIE   It wasn't funny Rob.

ROB   I know Susie. It was wrong.

SUSIE   It was fucking embarrassing, that's what it was. You know Luke was ready to land one on you don't you?

ROB   I know.

SUSIE   He wasn't impressed.

ROB   And I'm sorry. I didn't mean it.

SUSIE   You said a lot of stuff last night you shouldn't have Rob. And you said it all in front of Luke. That's what gets me. In front of him. You know how important he is to me.

ROB   Sorry.

SUSIE   I thought you were freaking out. I didn't know what was happening.

Rob goes to speak. Susie interrupts.

SUSIE   Just promise me you won't do it again all right? Don't you ever, ever, scare me like that again. Ok?

ROB   Ok.

SUSIE   But that doesn't mean I've let you off mind. I'm still not happy. And that goes for Luke and all.

ROB   I'll speak to him later. *(Beat)* How's it going?

SUSIE   Brilliantly, thank you very much for asking. Y'know, I think I might've landed myself a decent one at last. He's gorgeous looking, funny, and he hasn't got a single hang up. Touch wood.

ROB   Good.

SUSIE   He's been trying to get me to give this up y'know?

ROB   The show?

SUSIE   Wants me to stop ripping off sad old has-beens and start doing my own stuff. Singing as myself. Singing my own songs.

ROB   Will you?

SUSIE   I'm thinking about it.

ROB   Scary eh?

SUSIE   Skidmarks from here to Swansea and back mate. *(Beat)* What about Marky? Have you made it up with him?

ROB   Was it bad?

SUSIE   Well I didn't think I'd see him round the flat this morning if that's what you mean. Whatever's going on, you've got to sort it out Rob. You can't go through another night like last night.

ROB   I know. A lot's been going on lately. Too much.

SUSIE   What? Been arguing over whose turn it is to go on top again have you?

ROB   Steven came over to see me.

SUSIE   You're joking me? What brought him crawling back?

ROB   He's tested HIV positive.

Susie laughs.

SUSIE   I know you're a sick bastard Rob, but that is really low. Too low even for you. You shouldn't joke around with stuff like that.

No response.

SUSIE   Piss off Rob!

ROB   He came round to tell me. He thought I'd want to know.

SUSIE   No Rob. He can't be.

ROB   He thinks I should get a test done too. Just to make sure I'm negative.

SUSIE   Rob. No.

ROB   Just to make sure I'm negative Susie. Just to be safe. But I'm not going to. I mean, I reckon you'd know if there was something like that wrong with you? You'd feel it wouldn't you? *(Beat)* And anyway, who wants to know if they've got it? Who wants to live with that? I'd rather carry on not knowing for as long as I could, you know? Get stuck in and enjoy life while I still can? I couldn't find out that there was something major wrong with me like that and then just get on with things. Business as usual like. I don't see how you can get on with the ordinary stuff, the good stuff, knowing that one day you're going to get sick. Knowing that one day soon you might lose control, start falling apart, breaking down. *(Beat)* I'm scared Susie. So scared that I can't go. I can't get tested. I'm only twenty-four Susie. Things like this aren't supposed to happen.

The sounds of the sea against the shore builds up again, and continues into the next scene.

8. *Lights rise on Steven standing alone.*

STEVEN   The raft is fragile. It could break. Do all that you can to keep it together, and if the raft is strong, then it will pull you through. It has to.

9. *Lights up on the bathroom. Morning. Rob is shaving his face with a razor at the sink. Mark enters.*

MARK   You going out?

ROB   Nah, I just thought it was time to get rid of the designer stubble.

Spotting a heap of damp towels on the floor.

MARK   This bathroom's a bit of a tip.

Mark starts to tidy up.

ROB   Having four people living here isn't helping matters is it?

MARK   What d'you mean?

ROB   Luke. He's hardly the tidiest guy in the world is he?

MARK   He's all right.

ROB   Mark, he hasn't spent one night at his own place since he and Susie got together. He might as well move his stuff in and start paying rent if they're going to carry on like this.

MARK   Things'll settle.

ROB   Yeah, well, clearing up after him is the last thing on my mind at the moment.

MARK   When I saw you shaving there I thought you might've been planning on going down to the clinic.

ROB   Mark. Don't. Please.

MARK   I'm only saying that I thought you might've changed your mind.

ROB   Well I haven't.

MARK   You haven't considered it?

Rob cuts himself with the razor.

ROB   Fuck!

MARK   What? Are you all right?

ROB   Yeah. It's just a nick.

MARK   Come here.

Mark presses some tissue paper against the cut.

MARK   You should be more careful.

ROB   Yeah, and you shouldn't nag me. I was distracted.

MARK   I don't nag.

ROB   No?

MARK   No. I make useful suggestions.

ROB   I'm not stubborn y'know?

MARK   No?

ROB   Just because I don't talk about something all day long doesn't mean that I'm not thinking about it.

MARK   I know.

ROB   I do consider all the options.

MARK   I know. Look, just hold that there for five minutes, will you? Quietly.

ROB   Mark? Thanks.

Susie enters carrying shopping bags.

SUSIE   Good morning girls! Look what Susie's been up to.

MARK   Shopping?

SUSIE   Got it in one.

MARK   But it isn't even eleven o'clock yet.

SUSIE   So? It's never too early to go shopping. Not when you've got a lovely boyfriend who's prepared to exercise his credit card for you it isn't anyway.

ROB   Makes you sick doesn't it?

SUSIE   Jealous.

ROB   Well? What's he bought you then?

SUSIE   *(Opening one of the bags and pulling out a dress.)* Exhibit A. What d'you reckon?

ROB   It's lovely.

SUSIE   Yeah, I know. And there's some shoes to go with it, and a little something to go under it too.

ROB   Little being the operative word.

SUSIE   Oi. I'll have you know that small is beautiful.

ROB   You've changed your tune.

MARK   Where is moneybags anyway?

ROB   Arranging an overdraft by the look of it.

SUSIE   Unloading the car. I couldn't carry everything in by myself. And with him around, why should I?

ROB   There's more?

SUSIE   You look surprised. *(Beat)* Ooh. What've you done to your face bach?

ROB   Cut it shaving.

SUSIE You're joking aren't you? You should see my legs. *(Beat)* Come on. Quick fashion show'll soon make it better.

Luke appears in the door.

SUSIE   Talk of the devil.

ROB   Feeling generous Luke?

LUKE   She had me in an arm lock. What could I do?

SUSIE   You love it really. And I loves you.

Susie steals a kiss.

SUSIE   Ta darling. *(To Rob)* Now come and have a look. I've got this wonderful black top that's got buttons all up the sleeve and a neck....

Susie and Rob exit.

LUKE   She needed a few things.

MARK   Yeah. I saw.

LUKE   What you doing?

MARK   Just tidying the place up a bit.

LUKE   Sorry. That was me. In a bit of a rush, y'know?

Luke closes the door a little.

LUKE   Here. I'll give you a hand. *(Pause)* You're lucky you didn't go into town this morning. It was swarming. I've never seen so many people in one place before running from shop to shop like maniacs. You'd swear Queen Street was about to be demolished. Susie enjoyed herself though. As you probably saw from all the carriers.

MARK   Does this mean that you're planning on sticking around then? You've decided to stay with Susie?

LUKE   Yeah, it does.

MARK   Good.

LUKE   It is isn't it? And anyway, after the beating she gave my credit cards this morning I doubt if I could afford to get off anywhere else just yet. I like her Mark. I like her a lot. For the first time, in a long time, I'm happy here. I can see it now. I like what I'm doing, I like who I am, I like Susie, I like the friends I'm making, I like it all. So I've decided to go along with it. Stop running for a change.

MARK   Sounds deep.

LUKE   Does it? Well, as long as it doesn't sound wanky I'm not bothered.

MARK   I'm pleased for you Luke.

LUKE   Ta. I think this might well be it. Me and Susie. I think I've found what I want at last.

MARK   I'm glad.

Pause.

LUKE   What about you? Feeling better?

MARK   Yes thanks. Much.

LUKE   Good.

MARK   Thanks for putting up with me last night Luke.

LUKE   No worries. After all, it's meant to be good to talk isn't it?

MARK   Ta anyway. You were great.

LUKE   'Great?' I don't know about that. I'm not very good when it comes to dishing out advice, especially after a couple of drinks.

MARK   Whatever. Thank you.

LUKE   All I did was sit there. All I did was listen.

MARK   Well, you kissed me.

LUKE   Yeah, yeah there was that and all, wasn't there? And I'm not exactly sure why I did that. I mean, I don't make a habit of kissing blokes. As you know, it's not my thing. Men like. But last night, when you started crying, well, I didn't know what I was s'posed to do. I told you before, I'm a total fart when someone starts balling their eyes out on me, so, so, I kissed you. I wanted to make it better.

MARK   I know.

LUKE   That's the first time I've ever kissed a man too.

MARK   And? Did you like it?

LUKE   Well I can't say I'll be queuing up to have another shot at it in a hurry. Too many bristles for my liking.

MARK   Thanks Luke.

LUKE   What for?

MARK   Making me laugh.

LUKE   That's all right. That's what friends are for. And you can never have too many friends now can you Mark? *(Beat)* Serious though. If you ever want to talk to me, you can y'know? I won't mind. I want to be a mate.

Mark offers Luke a hand. They shake hands.

LUKE   Come here.

Luke pulls Mark into an embrace, and the door swings open a moment later to reveal Susie posing in her new dress and accessories. She looks far too glamorous, a little ridiculous, like one of her stage acts. The men release each other and then notice her.

SUSIE   What....? What....? What's going on in here then?

LUKE   Susie?

SUSIE   What're you doing? What in fuck's name do you two think you're playing at eh?

LUKE   It's nothing Susie.

SUSIE   Huh.

LUKE   We weren't doing anything. Come off it Susie. You don't reckon we were....?

SUSIE   Stranger things have happened.

LUKE   Come on Susie. You know I'm not queer.

SUSIE   Yeah. Right. So what were you doing pressed up against Mark like that then? Trying to measure his body temperature?

LUKE   I was only giving him a hug Susie. Just a hug. Nothing else.

SUSIE   Right? Hug all your friends like that do you?

LUKE   No.

SUSIE   Exactly.

LUKE   But it was just a hug Susie. That's all.

SUSIE   A hug?

LUKE   Yeah. A hug.

SUSIE   Nothing else? You sure you haven't been seeing each other on the sly? Meeting up at night for a quick snog? Going into the kitchen and playing with each other when no one was looking? Eh? Well?

Silence. Susie suddenly gets more serious.

SUSIE   What about you Mark? What d'you have to say about it? Huh! Was he good? Was he big enough for you? Nice and hard?

LUKE   I don't believe this.

SUSIE   Join the club. Oh sorry, I forgot. It looks like you already have.

MARK   Susie. He's right. We didn't do anything.

SUSIE   Was that because I walked in on you when I did, or what then?

MARK   For God's sake Susie! All he did was kiss me!

Pause.

SUSIE   What? He kissed you? Luke kissed you?

LUKE   It wasn't like that.

SUSIE   First of all he's hugging you, and now he's kissing you! Are you sure he didn't slip his hand down your boxers? Grab hold of your dick and start sucking you off as well? Or is that something else that's maybe slipped your mind?

LUKE   Susie. You've got it wrong.

SUSIE   I should've known. After all Mark? Isn't it about time you started looking for a new model? Wouldn't you prefer another boyfriend now instead of Rob? Fully working? Undamaged? Clean like my Luke?

Rob enters.

SUSIE   Don't tell me you haven't thought it Mark. Don't tell me you haven't thought about looking elsewhere, moving on. Not now, not now that you know Rob's HIV positive.

ROB   Susie! Stop it!

SUSIE   Well? It's true isn't it? You're positive?

LUKE   What?

ROB   I haven't tested. We don't know that yet.

LUKE   He's HIV positive?

SUSIE   *(Gradually becoming more distressed.)* But why haven't you tested Rob? Why haven't you gone and found out? It's because you already know isn't it? And this is just your little way of putting off telling everyone the truth. *(Beat)* Here's the plan see Mark, Rob goes round telling everyone that he hasn't tested, that he won't test, because there's nothing to worry about, and then he doesn't have to face it, he doesn't have to tell everyone that he's ill, that he's got it, and that he's going to get Aids!

MARK   *(Reaching out to calm her down.)* Susie....

SUSIE *(Fighting him off.)* Fuck off! Get the fuck off me!

ROB Susie....

SUSIE *(Holding onto Rob. Distraught.)* No. I don't give a shit. I don't care anymore. I can't handle it. I can't do this anymore Rob. I'm sorry, but I can't, I can't do this. I can't deal with it. I'm so sorry.

Susie exits. Pause. Feeling uncomfortable, Luke follows her.

MARK Rob.....

ROB Yeah. I know.

Sounds of the sea against the shore build up again and continue over into the next scene.

10. *Lights rise on Steven standing alone.*

STEVEN   Two men decided to build a raft. They built it well and made sure that it was strong enough to carry them through the roughest water.

And when it was ready, when they could do no more, the two men carried it down to the shore, and laid it on the water.

11. *A beach. Early evening. The sound of waves, seagulls, etc. Rob is standing looking out to sea. Mark comes in a moment later.*

ROB   We used to come down here all the time when we were kids, even in the middle of winter. We'd park up there and Dad'd get us chips from the van and a can of Coke to share with a straw each.   And we'd whinge about it.   We'd whine about coming down here and just sitting, just sitting for hours inside the car. And when she couldn't stand the whingeing anymore, Mum would turn round and tell us to sit quietly and watch the waves, as though they were doing something unusual.   Dad loved it though.   He'd stare out through the windscreen - transfixed. Watching the waves stamp their way in and out, the strangers walking their dogs across the wet sand. *(Beat)* He never got round to it but he always wanted to move down here. He was forever talking about buying a caravan up on the bank, somewhere where he could watch the sea from the window.

MARK   It's getting late.

ROB   What's going to happen Mark?

MARK   What d'you want to happen?

ROB   I want you to stay with me.

MARK   I can't stay unless you go down and test Rob. I want you to go and find out what's happening. I need to know.

ROB   And what if I am positive?

MARK   I have to know Rob. We have to find out so that we know what to do. So we can make it better.

ROB   Dad used to walk down here almost every weekend. He'd come down by himself sometimes and walk right up to the water's edge, just far enough so the water'd skim the front of his shoes.

MARK   Will you test Rob?

ROB   Yes, if you'll walk down to the water with me. I want to get my feet wet.

Rob offers his hand to Mark. He comes forward and accepts it. They hold hands and walk away.

12. *Dressing room of a club. Susie is sitting at a dressing table getting ready to go out on stage. We can hear noises from the club in the background. Luke appears.*

SUSIE   Well? Are they ready for me?

LUKE   When you are.

SUSIE   And they know what order I'm doing the songs in? They know my cue?

LUKE   Don't worry about it. It's sorted. *(Beat)* How're you feeling?

SUSIE   Honestly? Shit scared.

LUKE   You'll be fine.

SUSIE   Easy to say. You're not the one going out onto that stage. Yeah well, the first time's always the worst. It's the same old story when you try something different, isn't it? Especially since they're not getting what they're expecting. Since it's just me tonight. Plain old Susie.

LUKE   Just go out there as yourself. Show them what you can do. Five minutes yeah?

Luke turns to the door and goes. Susie carries on applying her make-up, and then looks up.

SUSIE   *(Smiling.)* What? Don't I even get a goodbye kiss?

13. *Bathroom. Morning. Bright sunshine pours in. Rob is at the sink washing his face, combing his hair etc. Mark appears in the doorway and watches him for a few seconds.*

MARK   Aren't you ready yet?

ROB   Five more minutes I promise.

MARK   You've been in here all morning, what've you been doing?

ROB   Some essential plumbing. What d'you think?

MARK   I see Susie's cleared out the last of her stuff then?

ROB   Yeah. She left her keys on the table.

Mark approaches Rob from behind and puts his arms around him.

MARK   So we've got the place all to ourselves?   You know what this means don't you?

ROB   Double the rent?

MARK   *(Playfully)* You're such a romantic bastard aren't you? You've got sixty seconds Rob. Sixty seconds and I'm going without you.

Mark exits. Buttoning his shirt, Rob goes over to the window and looks out. After a moment, he closes his eyes, and stretches his arms out, enjoying the glorious sunlight. Pause. Mark comes back in with Rob's jacket.

MARK   What are you doing?

ROB   Nothing. I was just watching all the cars passing by. Like nothing had happened.

Mark goes over to the window.

MARK   Yeah. It's a beautiful day.

14. *Lights rise on Steven standing alone. We can still see Mark and Rob in the bathroom, motionless. Sound of waves crashing against the shore.*

STEVEN   And when they laid it on the water - it floated - it sailed.

Fades.

Keiron Self, Roland Powell   *photo: Brian Tarr*

Lowri Mae, Keiron Self   *photo: Brian Tarr*

Gulp

Roland Powell

photo: Brian Tarr

My Piece of Happiness

Lewis Davies

My Piece of Happiness was premiéred by Made in Wales at Chapter, Cardiff, in January 1998 with the following cast.

Sean	James Westaway
George	Dorien Thomas
Sarah / Mrs.Grigeli	Lowri Mae
Mrs.Evans / Angel	Sharon Morgan
Hospital Orderly / Test / Jazz fan / Collins	David Middleton

Directed by	**Jeff Teare**
Designed by	**Carolyn Willitts**
Lighting by	**Ceri James**
Assistant Director	**Rebecca Gould**

Scene 1:

Lights come up on a park bench. A wire bin, half-filled with rubbish stands to one side. Sean hurries into the park, scanning the exits but not appearing to see anyone. He struggles with a large paper-sack which he lifts onto his lap when he reaches the bench. He begins to carefully count the newspapers inside his sack. George saunters into the scene. He also has a bag slung around his shoulders. He is edging through middle age but there is a resilient toughness to his appearance that is not softened by a worn black leather jacket. He sits down on the bench next to Sean.

GEORGE: Awright ?

SEAN: Yeh.

GEORGE: Finished ?

SEAN: Yes George.

GEORGE: Quick ?

SEAN: *(Nods.)*

GEORGE: You got any left ?

SEAN: *(Signals yes)*

GEORGE: How many ?

SEAN: Twelve, I've got twelve left, I had forty five to start with

George, now I've got twelve.

GEORGE: Well we've got fifteen then because I've got three.

SEAN: I didn't miss any out George.

GEORGE: Yeh ?

SEAN: I delivered them all.

GEORGE: Why do you think we've got papers over then ?

SEAN: I don't know George, I've got twelve and you've got three, that's fifteen. — Why do you think we've got fifteen over George?

GEORGE: Did you do all the flats ?

SEAN: All of them George.

GEORGE: What about the Close ?

SEAN: Did that George.

GEORGE: Well we've got fifteen left. Are you sure you didn't miss any out?

SEAN: I didn't George, I delivered all mine, I wouldn't miss any out George, I counted them all. *(Desperate to convince him.)*

GEORGE: You counted them all ?

SEAN: I did George, all of them, all the houses on my side.

GEORGE: You sure ?

SEAN: Even down The Close George. Nine houses.

GEORGE: Perhaps Collins gave us too many then ?

SEAN: *(Seizes on it.)* Yes George he must have, that's what he did, because I didn't miss any, I counted all mine.

GEORGE: We'll just have to tell him won't we ?

SEAN: Yeh George. — You'll tell him, won't you ? You'll tell Mr.Collins ?

GEORGE: Yes I'll tell him Sean.
Silence as Sean counts his papers again.

SEAN: We've always got papers over George.

GEORGE: Aye, I know that.

SEAN: Mrs.Eynon said hello to me George.

GEORGE: Did she invite you in for tea ?

SEAN: I didn't go in this time George, I know we've got to finish. I got to get home by six.

GEORGE: You mother'll be expecting you.

SEAN: She will George, she gets worried when I'm not home.

GEORGE: How is your mother Sean ?

SEAN: She's fine George. — The doctor came on Saturday night.

GEORGE: He did ?

SEAN: Yeh he did. But Mam's alright now. She was out of bed again yesterday.

GEORGE: Is the nurse still coming in the mornings ?

SEAN: Yes, she still comes to get Mam up, she's lovely Aunty Margaret.

GEORGE: How's your Dad ?

SEAN: He's great, he took me to the football on Saturday, but we lost and he wasn't very happy. On Sunday he told me to keep out of his way because of his head. I think he'd been drinking.

GEORGE: Your Dad likes a drink, does he ?

SEAN: Sometimes George he likes it so much when we win he has to stay out. He sends me home in a taxi.

GEORGE: On your own ?

SEAN: My mother doesn't like that though. She doesn't like him staying out on his own.

GEORGE: He took you home Saturday though ?

SEAN: Yes. He said Mam wasn't very well. And then the doctor came. He's like that my Dad, he knows things.

GEORGE: Sean, about your mother.

SEAN: Yes?

GEORGE: She's very ill.

SEAN: I know that. The doctor came. Mum said she'd be alright now.

GEORGE: Sometimes Sean when people are ill , — they don't get better.

SEAN: Yes I know that George, but my mother will, she's my mother.

GEORGE: Sean ? It's — one thing —

SEAN: Yes George ?

GEORGE: How's the centre ?

SEAN: It's good George. I'm learning everything there.

GEORGE: Aye. *(George drifts.)*

SEAN: Mr.Test thinks I'm doing really well.

GEORGE: He should know.

SEAN: He says when I have my report like, it'll be good.

GEORGE: You still making more friends there ?

SEAN: Yeh, lots of them.

GEORGE: *(Nods head.)*

SEAN: Some I don't like though. Some are stupid.

GEORGE: You get 'em like that.

SEAN: *(Begins to speak, then stops himself, starts again, stops.)*.

GEORGE: Go on, what are you going to say ?

SEAN: Nothing.

GEORGE: Go on mun.

SEAN: I've got a girlfriend.

GEORGE: 'Ave you ?

SEAN: I have, her name's Sarah Evans.

GEORGE: Where did you meet her then ?

SEAN: I met her at the centre, she's lovely.

GEORGE: I'm sure she is.

SEAN: She's twenty three.

GEORGE: Yeh, how long have you known her then ?

SEAN: She's been there before me. Like a couple of years I think. But we're going out now.

GEORGE: Am I going to meet her ?

SEAN: I dunno, I only see her at the centre, you could call over George if you like.

GEORGE: Yeh perhaps I will.

SEAN: Wednesday. When we go on the bus.

GEORGE: Why don't you take her out on the weekend then ?

SEAN: Her mother won't let her.

GEORGE: Aw c'mon, I'm sure she will.

SEAN: No she won't, she's only allowed to the centre.

GEORGE: You sure ?

SEAN: Yeh I'm sure George, Sarah told me.

GEORGE: Do you want to take her out on the weekend ?

SEAN: She won't be allowed. And where could I take her ?

GEORGE: What you doing week Saturday ?

SEAN: Football's over George. But she's not allowed.

GEORGE: I tell you what, I'll have a word with Mr. Test at the centre and I'll see if I can persuade him to talk to her mother.

SEAN: Where can I take her George?

GEORGE: Don't worry about that I'll take you both out in my car.

SEAN: That would be great George.

GEORGE: What's her name again ?

SEAN: I told you, Sarah Evans.

GEORGE: I know but I forgot. I'm useless with names.

SEAN: Would you really take us out ?

GEORGE: Yeh sure, if I can.

SEAN: You won't forget ?

GEORGE: No.

SEAN: Saturday then ?

GEORGE: Well don't get your hopes up but we'll see what we can do. *(Looks around then stands.)*

SEAN: I won't George, Saturday right ?

GEORGE: Week Saturday.

SEAN: Yeh.

GEORGE: I'll talk to Mr. Test.

SEAN: And her mother ?

GEORGE: Mr. Test will.

SEAN: Not this Saturday, next Saturday.

GEORGE: You ready ?

SEAN: What for ?

GEORGE: To go home.

SEAN: Yeh sure George.

GEORGE: C'mon or your mother will be wondering where you are, give me the rest of your papers. *(Sean passes him his newspapers which he folds with his excess and then promptly drops in the bin.)*
Don't want Collins to think we didn't deliver them all do we ?

SEAN: No we don't George.

SEAN'S VIGIL I:
A short visual scene variations of which recur throughout the play. A TV is tuned to the static and now represents one of two points of light on an otherwise dark stage. Opposite the TV a chair waits for a viewer. Sean appears out of the shadows and sits; intently watching the screen from which there is no sound. A bright light focuses, drawing his colour. The scene holds, there is a peel of laughter from beyond the stage followed by a playful scream; street noises. Then darkness.

Scene II:
A young woman looks into a dressing table mirror. She is applying finishing touches with make-up. The process is frustrating her. She speaks quietly to herself.

MRS.EVANS: *(Not in room.)* Sarah ?

SARAH: *(Leans closer to the mirror.)*

MRS.EVANS: Sarah are you ready yet ?

SARAH: No not yet.

MRS.EVANS: Sarah, the gentlemen will be here at twelve.

SARAH: I'm not ready yet.

MRS.EVANS: It's not polite to keep them waiting.

SARAH: Sean don't mind waiting.

MRS.EVANS: That's not the point.

SARAH: He's always late anyway.

MRS.EVANS: How do you know that ?

SARAH: *(Shrugs shoulders.)*

MRS.EVANS: Sarah ?

SARAH: He just is. He's always last. Swimming, dinner time. Everything.

MRS.EVANS: Perhaps today he'll be on time.

SARAH: Ahhh. *(frustrated)*

MRS.EVANS: Shall I help you Sarah ?

SARAH: I can do it.

MRS.EVANS: Just take your time, it'll come.

MRS.EVANS: Is Sean new to the centre ?

SARAH: He's been there a year.

MRS.EVANS: You've never mentioned him before.

SARAH: I haven't been seeing him before have I ?

MRS.EVANS: You should have told me about him.

SARAH: Why ?

MRS.EVANS: You know your father doesn't like surprises.

SARAH: He's okay Sean. Dad'll like him. He's got a job.

MRS.EVANS: A job ?

SARAH: He has. He delivers papers. Him and Mr.Rees.

MRS.EVANS: I thought Mr.Rees worked at the centre ?

SARAH: No he delivers papers with Sean. Every Thursday. —
I think he might have another job as well.

MRS.EVANS: I hope so.

SARAH: Where they taking me ?

MRS.EVANS: I told you, it's a surprise.

SARAH: I want to go to the beach.

MRS.EVANS: It's too cold for the beach.

SARAH: The beach next week then.

MRS.EVANS: Next week is it ?

SARAH: He's my boyfriend. I like him.

MRS.EVANS: Yes we'll see.

SARAH: I can have a boyfriend can't I ?

MRS.EVANS: You know you can Sarah.

SARAH: And Dad won't mind ?

MRS.EVANS: You've had a boyfriend before.

SARAH: I've never been out before.

MRS.EVANS: You've never asked.

SARAH: Dad would have said no.

MRS.EVANS: You're older now.

SARAH: Does that make a difference?

MRS.EVANS: Of course it does.

SARAH: How?

MRS.EVANS: You can do other things. Grown up things.

SARAH: Like what?

MRS.EVANS: You're going out on your own on a Saturday afternoon. That's what you can do.

SARAH: Is that all ?

MRS.EVANS: Isn't that enough ?

SARAH: I want to do more.

MRS.EVANS: But this is a new thing for you. You can't do it all at once.

SARAH: I'm old enough.

MRS.EVANS: I've told you that. But there's no rush.

SARAH: I want to go out every night and...

MRS.EVANS: You'll be able to see him again.

SARAH: I will?

MRS.EVANS: Yes, if you like him.

SARAH: I like him a lot. He's my boyfriend. You had a boyfriend didn't you ?

MRS.EVANS: Yes once.

SARAH: Is he still your boyfriend?

MRS.EVANS: He's your father.

SARAH: Dad's your boyfriend ?

MRS.EVANS: He is.

SARAH: He's too old to be a boyfriend.

MRS.EVANS: We've got older.

SARAH: Nah, don't believe you.

MRS.EVANS: When you get older you get married.

SARAH: I could get married.

MRS.EVANS: Why would you want to do a thing like that ?

SARAH: So I could live with someone.

MRS.EVANS: You don't need to do that. You live with us.

SARAH: Yeh I could still get married though and live with you.

MRS.EVANS: I'm not sure your father would be too keen on that idea.

SARAH: But I'm older now.

MRS.EVANS: You're always rushing —

Sarah screams in frustration with the mirror.

MRS.EVANS: Come here Sarah.

Sarah turns reluctantly from the mirror on the table.

MRS.EVANS: You need to take your time a bit more. (*Brushes the lipstick into place.*) There. You look lovely Sarah.

Scene III
Saturday afternoon. Cosmeston country park.
George wanders on, he is carrying a haversack and a pair of binoculars hang around his neck. He appears to wait for someone. Sean and Sarah follow him. They meander around shyly.

GEORGE: Here we are then folks, on the lakes. Like it here ?

SEAN: Yeh George, its good.

SARAH: I like the water Mr.Rees.

GEORGE: Call me George mun love, I don't know who Mr.Rees is.

SEAN: You're Mr.Rees

GEORGE: Yeh I know that. What do you call me ?

SEAN: George.

GEORGE: Well there you are then.

SARAH: Nice of you to bring us George.

GEORGE: Nice to be out on a Saturday.

SEAN: I like to go the football on a Saturday. My Dad takes me.

GEORGE: I thought the season has finished ?

SEAN: It has now George. But next year perhaps we can all go to the football.

SARAH: Are you going to take us out every Saturday Mr.Rees ?

GEORGE: You won't want to come with me every week I'm sure.

SEAN: Why George ?

GEORGE: I don't want to be with me every Saturday but I ain't got no choice in the matter.

SEAN: What do you mean George ?

GEORGE: You'll be wanting to go out on your own and things.

SARAH: My mother won't like that Mr.Rees, you'll have to come to.

GEORGE: Aren't we thinking a bit much here good people. We're out today. Now.

SARAH: Its lovely Mr.Rees. The water. Very nice of you to bring us Mr.Rees.

SEAN: Call him George, Sarah.

SARAH: (*Looks sharply at Sean.*)

GEORGE: Never mind, you call me what you like. I'll answer to it.

SEAN: Are we going to eat now ?

GEORGE: Sure if you want to. The sandwiches and stuff are in here. Are you hungry Sarah ?

SARAH: (*Shrugs shoulders.*) Sure Mr.Rees

GEORGE: I'll leave you to the food. I'm not that hungry yet and someone told me there's Grebes on the far side.

SEAN: (*To Sarah*) ?

SARAH: (*Shrugs shoulders*).

GEORGE: You'll be alright here won't you ? No swimming now.

SEAN: What about your sandwiches George ?
GEORGE: Don't worry about me I'll have some when I get back.

SEAN: Okay George, we'll stay right here, we won't go anywhere.

George ambles off; they shuffle nervously around still holding hands.

SEAN: Do you want a sandwich ?

SARAH: No.

SEAN: George made them.

SARAH: I'm not hungry.

SEAN: Nor me.

SARAH: We can eat later.

SEAN: Yeh. — Do you like George ?

SARAH: Yeh he seems nice. I seen him at the centre sometimes.

SEAN: He's my mate George is, we work together on the papers, you know, my job ? I told you ?

SARAH: On a Thursday ?

SEAN: Yeh that's the one. I get paid for it.

SARAH: How much ?

SEAN: Fifteen pounds.

SARAH: Really ?

SEAN: George says I don't even need to pay tax if I keep it quiet.

SARAH: My Dad pays tax.

SEAN: I don't. I keep all my money. That's what George says.

SARAH: Did you miss any out this week ?

SEAN: Sssh mun, someone might be listening.

SARAH: Don't be silly.

SEAN: I had nine left.

SARAH: You must have missed some houses then.

SEAN: I counted them all.

SARAH: But you had some over.

GEORGE: You won't tell George will you ? — You won't ?

SARAH: No of course not.

GEORGE: 'Cos I don't want to lose it.

SARAH: I'm not going to tell anyone.

She smiles at Sean; who makes an attempt at kissing her but rushes at it and botches it. He turns away in embarrassment.

SEAN: Sorry.

SARAH: What for?

SEAN: I don't know.

SARAH: Put the rug down so we can sit on the grass.

SEAN: I'll put the rug down.

Sarah sits on the rug, kicking off her shoes, she pushes out her stocking covered toes. Sean just looks at her.

SARAH: C'mon then.

Sean looks at Sarah dumbly before joining her on the rug. His arm drifts shyly around her shoulder. She turns and confidently kisses him on the lips. She holds the kiss and pushes him back on the grass.

SEAN'S VIGIL II
The TV is now tuned to the twilight zone between the static and signal; there is accompanying sound. Sean takes the viewing seat; he discards a used chip paper. The scene holds for ten seconds.

Scene IV
Secure wing of mental handicap hospital ward.
An orderly sits reading a paper. There are shouts from the distance but no people. The orderly doesn't react.
George enters the ward. Stands above the orderly.

ORD: Can I 'elp you mate ?

GEORGE: Sean Dent, I'm his keyworker.

ORD: Not sure.

GEORGE: Admitted Sunday. Bereavement emergency ?

ORD: Oh yeh, Sean Dent. I think he's out in the garden.

GEORGE: Garden ?

ORD: Yeh there's a garden at the back of the ward.

George nods. The ord returns to his paper.

GEORGE: How's he been ?

ORD: Fine, fine.

GEORGE: Settling in okay ?

ORD: Yeh.

GEORGE: Anything else ?

ORD: Anything else what ?

GEORGE: Has he been upset, nervous ? Other obvious signs of distress ?

ORD: How do I know mate ? This isn't an observation unit. What do you want a progress report ?

GEORGE: That would be extremely helpful.

ORD: Why don't you ask the staff nurse ?

The orderly returns to his paper. George thinks about leaving, then leans over the orderly's shoulder.

GEORGE: Anything good in the paper ?

ORD: What ?

GEORGE: Useful information, spiritual guidance on how to live life?

ORD: It's all rubbish mate.

GEORGE: Has it got a TV page?

ORD: Yeh they all have, why ?

GEORGE: Sport ?

ORD: At the back.

GEORGE: Crossword any good ?

ORD: What you on about?

GEORGE: Just passing time.

ORD: I told you where he is.

GEORGE: (*Leans close to the orderly.*)   Do you enjoy your job?

ORD: Hey,

GEORGE: Well ?

ORD: Who do you think you are ?

GEORGE: I told you I'm his keyworker, assessment officer, paper deliverer, ex-boxer. Friend.

ORD: So ?

GEORGE: I expect a bit more co-operation from a fellow professional.

ORD: There's only so much we can do.

GEORGE: And I only have this amount of patience left.

ORD: I'll get one of the other nurses to talk to you. I wasn't on when he was admitted.

GEORGE: That would be an excellent idea. (*Orderly begins to walk off.*) And find out about his medication while you are there. Stress can change his behaviour, awright ?

Scene V
George finds the garden. Sean sits alone on a seat.

GEORGE: Hello.

SEAN: George, George how, how are you here ?

GEORGE: I'm here to see you aren't I ?

SEAN: George, to see me, you've come up to see me George ?

GEORGE: 'Course I have.

SEAN: Thanks George.

GEORGE: That's alright mun, you're my mate.

SEAN: Really George ?

GEORGE: 'Course.

SEAN: I'm your mate too George, honest I am. I'm you're mate on the papers right ?

GEORGE: That's right.

SEAN: I don't like it here George. It's not nice.

GEORGE: No, I guess it's not.

SEAN: I don't like it here.

GEORGE: You're okay though aren't you, no-one's touched you or anything ?

SEAN: Not nice George. Not nice. Don't want to stay here long George. Want to go back home .

GEORGE: Can't go back right now Sean. You might have to stay here a few days.

SEAN: Want to go home.

GEORGE: Your Dad, your Dad can't cope too well on his own. He's old see and he's missing your mother.

SEAN: My mother George ? She's gone hasn't she ?

GEORGE: Yes.

SEAN: They said she was going to get better George. They said, they promised. But she's not is she George ? She's not going to get any better ?

GEORGE: No she's not. She can't get better now. Your mother was very ill, in a lot of pain. You know that don't you ?

SEAN: She's out of pain now George, my Dad said that ?

GEORGE: He's right Sean. The pain's over now. No more.

SEAN: George ?

GEORGE: Aye ?

SEAN: George when people die right ? When they die they're buried right ? In the churchyard like my Gran ?

GEORGE: That's right

SEAN: Are they putting Mam there ? In the churchyard ?

GEORGE: Yes, I think so.

SEAN: Right. — George has your mother ever died ?

GEORGE: I'm er, not sure, probably by now.

SEAN: Did they put her in the churchyard George ?

GEORGE: I like to think so Sean. Somewhere warm by the sea perhaps.

SEAN: You'd be upset too wouldn't you ?

GEORGE: Chocolate ?

SEAN: Thank you George. George ? Can't stay here George.

GEORGE: I don't think you'll have to stay long.

SEAN: (*He waves his friend closer*). The people, they look at me George, just stare. Don't say anything, then they laugh or scream, sometimes both. I think they're mad George.

GEORGE: They're not mad Sean.

SEAN: They could be George. You'd never know. Nutters.

GEORGE: Don't worry they're fine mate. Have another chocolate ?

SEAN: Thank you George.

Scene VI

Community Mental Handicap offices; Social Services. There is a typewriter and a box file on the round table. A faded poster of Che Guevara is visible on the wall as is a bust of Karl Marx. George is sitting at a window looking out. Angel is pacing the room, she is tall, thin and gives the impression that her body is constantly on the move. She checks her watch, her file which she clasps jealously to her chest and then the clock on the wall. George turns his gaze on her with a vague disinterest before reverting to the window. He is bored by her constant motion. A deteriorating grey man, MrTest, sits in one of the chairs fiddling with his pen and cufflinks.

ANGEL: It's almost two, they promised they would be here by one. I suppose we should have expected it really, the day after the funeral.

TEST: They'll have a few things to think about.

ANGEL: Still it's almost an hour. (*She checks her watch again and then continues pacing the room.*)

TEST: It's always a difficult time.

GEORGE: I think this is her now. No sign of Sean or his Dad.

ANGEL: His father must be coming ?

GEORGE: Doesn't look like it.

ANGEL: We can't get very far without him.

GEORGE: He's not with her.

ANGEL: I spoke to him yesterday morning.

GEORGE: What about Sean ?

ANGEL: I did try to insist that he should attend.

GEORGE: Just like the funeral.

ANGEL: They didn't think he needed to be there.

GEORGE: Or here by the looks of it.

ANGEL: It wasn't easy.

GEORGE: He should have attended.

TEST: The funeral I can understand.

GEORGE: Why ?

TEST: It can be upsetting.

GEORGE: It's a funeral.

ANGEL: I'll go and show her in.

Angel leaves.

TEST: Do you know the family George ?

GEORGE: Sort of, you know how it is. The mother made the decisions.

TEST: What about Mr.Dent?

GEORGE: He's alright. Nice enough bloke but he's been drunk for years.

TEST: It's always a shame.

GEORGE: Just another way out.

TEST: And *(Checks notes.)* MrsGrigeli is Sean's sister ?

GEORGE: Married with kids. I've met her once or twice.

TEST: Older than Sean then ?

GEORGE: Ten years or so.

TEST: Has she been supportive ?

GEORGE: She used to be more involved. Grew up with it all.

TEST: You spoken to her about the future ?

GEORGE: I don't really know her that well. Caught up with her own kids, but she's sharp. Used to go to the public meetings.

TEST: Really ?

GEORGE: She was close to her mother. Might decide Sean's all her responsibility or she may have had enough.

TEST: She can't just abandon him ?

GEORGE: What are we here for ?

TEST: I do dislike these changes. Unsettles everything. I had important work at The Centre this afternoon.

GEORGE: Oh yeh. And what was that ?

TEST: You wouldn't believe it George.

GEORGE: No.

TEST: I've got so many things to do.

ANGEL: Please come in.

Angel is leading a woman in her early thirties.

ANGEL: This is Mr.Test, he's the Training Centre manager.

TEST: Pleased to meet you. (*Struggles briefly to his feet.*)

ANGEL: And I think you may have met Sean's Assessment Officer, George Rees

GEORGE: Hello Mrs.Grigeli sorry to hear about your mother.

Grigeli just nods. Angel and Grigeli face each other.

ANGEL: Please take a seat Mrs.Grigeli. — May I first offer the condolences from the whole team on your mothers death. — Did the funeral go well ?

GRIGELI: As well as can be expected.

ANGEL: Good. — How is Sean ?

GRIGELI: I don't know, you tell me, he's in your hospital.

ANGEL: You haven't been to see him then ?

GRIGELI: When do you think I've had time ?

ANGEL: Of course, I was just concerned about him that's all.

GRIGELI: Well that's a revelation.

GEORGE: He's okay, I was with him yesterday, a bit shaken by the routine of the place but he insisted that he's going to turn up for the round tomorrow.

GRIGELI: Never mind about his bloody round.

GEORGE: It's important to him, he enjoys it.

GRIGELI: He enjoys it ?

GEORGE: And there's the money.

GRIGELI: He can hardly support himself on that, fifteen pound a week.

GEORGE: That's all he's allowed to earn or they'll stop his benefit.

GRIGELI: And where would we be without that ?

GEORGE: That's not the point, it's a job to him.

GRIGELI: Bloody great job that, delivering papers.

ANGEL: Perhaps we can get back to the purpose of the meeting.

GRIGELI: With pleasure. What are you going to do with him ?

ANGEL: Well that presents a difficulty at this time because obviously we haven't budgeted for the situation.
(Looks to Test for support but none is forthcoming.)

GRIGELI: And what does that mean ?

ANGEL: There is a limit on this year's assessment allocations.

We've missed the application date until the new assessment round is due to be re-assessed in the Autumn.

GRIGELI: You haven't got enough money for him ?

TEST: It's not that we haven't got any money it's just that it's all allocated in the wrong places at this present time.

GRIGELI: *(To Angel)* As I said you haven't got any money for him.

ANGEL: It has to be considered, the various options.

GRIGELI: Where's he going to go then ?

ANGEL: I was hoping Mr.Dent might have been able to attend.

GRIGELI: Why?

ANGEL: Legally Sean is still his responsibility.

GRIGELI: Don't you think my father has done enough ?

ANGEL: Of course under the present circumstances it would be unreasonable to ask your father to manage alone but with time and a bit of extra home support ?

GRIGELI: I can't have him. I've got two kids of my own. Sean is a lot of work.

ANGEL: I understand that.

GRIGELI: I don't think you do. You can't understand everything unless you're there.

ANGEL: No of course not...

GRIGELI: And my Dad hasn't been coping with my mother's illness. He's not at his best right now and Sean, sometimes makes it worse.

ANGEL: Would it be possible to discuss the problems with your father ?

GRIGELI: Why ?

ANGEL: So we can talk about what he needs in terms of support.

GRIGELI: My father doesn't want anything.

ANGEL: We could increase George's time and perhaps put someone in for a few hours in the mornings.

GRIGELI: A few hours in the mornings, have you ever had to look after Sean ? I assure you it's a round the clock job, it's not something that takes up a few hours in the mornings.

ANGEL: He does attend the day centre four days a week.

GRIGELI: And what's that, ten to four and then the bus drops him off and it's so long, see you tomorrow.

ANGEL: I still think it is an important service...

GRIGELI: What the hell does he do at the sodding day centre anyway ?

Her attack turns to Test, who despite his dugout defenses has been ambushed.

TEST: Er let me see. (*Desperately scrambles through his notes; eventually.*) Well Sean's involved in a number of programmes at the moment, there's the pottery, the dance class and oh yes, he goes swimming once a week.

GRIGELI: Pottery and dance, that's very appropriate that is, it's not exactly useful for him is it ?

TEST: We try to do our best with the limited resources available Mrs. Grigeli.

GRIGELI: Limited resources, it's always been the same bloody limited resources.

TEST: The Training centre has...

GRIGELI: You lot had the same excuse seven years ago. What were you running then ?

TEST: It had a different name then.

GRIGELI: That's all you've done.

TEST: There are a range of aims. We have to develop a general approach to training.

GRIGELI: Training him for what ? If he's not good enough to do anything then let's be honest about it.

TEST: We're not exactly a prority at the moment but we do have an application pending for more money.

GRIGELI: My brother's forgotten out there.

TEST: Mrs.Grigeli I can assure you it's not easy to get money out of the council under the present financial circumstances.

GRIGELI: Sean can't bloody do it can he ?

TEST: There are other considerations.

GRIGELI: What ? Your cosy little jobs ?

ANGEL: I do feel we're getting off the point here again Mrs.Grigeli.

GRIGELI: The point ? This is the point, Sean's life is the point.

GEORGE: Maybe we could find him a place at Andy's house.

He's got a spare room and they could split the bills.

ANGEL: There's nothing in Andy Day's plan about someone moving in with him.

GEORGE: He might like the company.

ANGEL: You're presuming a lot George.

GRIGELI: Who's Andy Day ?

ANGEL: Mr.Day is one of our other clients.

GRIGELI: And he has a Social Services house?

ANGEL: Er yes but..

GRIGELI: And there's room there?

ANGEL: Not necessarily but — *(Glances uneasily at Grigeli before turning briefly to her notes.)* Provisionally there might be some support available for a joint tenancy.

GRIGELI: Is it fully staffed ?

ANGEL: Mr.Day is one of our clients with high support needs.

GRIGELI: So he has a team of carers ?

ANGEL: Yes.

GRIGELI: Could it be expanded for my brother ?

ANGEL: It is possible we might be able to use the underspend money this year. This will all be provisional you understand.

GRIGELI: It usually is.

ANGEL: And perhaps put a formal bid in next year if the experiment is still working. Of course if it's what your father wants ?

GRIGELI: My father wants out.

ANGEL: Do you think your father would benefit from some counselling at this time ?

GRIGELI: No thank you. We've had enough strangers messing around in our lives.

ANGEL: It's a service Mrs.Grigeli, we can't do everything.

GRIGELI: My mother had to. She loved him but it was a life sentence. I can't. I've got my own life.

ANGEL: I understand the stress.

GRIGELI: No. No you don't. You just get him a house.
The commitment was ours but this is an end to it.

ANGEL: It still must be provisional.

GRIGELI: I'm not sure what you understand about my father but, if you know anything about his problems you know you can't put Sean back with him.

ANGEL: We'll still need to discuss changes with your father.

GRIGELI: He's not interested anymore.

ANGEL: He must be involved.

GRIGELI: Why ?

ANGEL: He's Sean's father.

GRIGELI: That's why he drinks.

ANGEL: I'm sorry.

GRIGELI: Don't be sorry, you can't be. Just sort it out.

ANGEL: Shall I contact you when we know further details of the arrangements ?

GRIGELI: How long will it take you ?

ANGEL: It's hard to say, maybe a fortnight. We'll need a few permissions. Will Mr.Dent agree to signing the necessary forms?

GRIGELI: He'll sign anything you ask him to.

ANGEL: Will you speaking to your father tonight ?

GRIGELI: My shift doesn't finish until ten. It'll have to be tomorrow.

ANGEL: I'll need to see him soon.

GRIGELI: The afternoons are best. He should be there.

ANGEL: Yes of course.

GRIGELI: I'm already late. Thank you for your time.

Grigeli leaves, George and Angel stand to show her out but do not leave. Silence as the fallout of the meeting settles on the remaining occupants of the room; Angel turns on George.

ANGEL: George I find that extremely unprofessional revealing a clients confidential information in a totally unrelated case.

GEORGE: Oh c'mon we had nowhere to go.

ANGEL: You put the whole service in an untenable position and compromised.....

GEORGE: How many nights would you like to spend in that hospital ?

ANGEL: That is not the issue.

GEORGE: I'm sorry I thought the meeting was about Sean's welfare.

ANGEL: That is not a very useful response, it would be helpful if you took some notice of the financial realities.

GEORGE: I'm his assessment officer.

ANGEL: And I've got thirty other families to think of. I was hoping that with extra support Mr.Dent could be persuaded to continue looking after him.

GEORGE: We always stretch the situation to breaking point don't we ? Put in the bare minimum to keep the family functioning, no matter at what level, just keep it functioning until it shatters and then we have to sweep up the pieces.

ANGEL: Very dramatic George but useless. Who the hell do you think you are ?

GEORGE: I think the family has gone, you heard her, they've served their sentence, it's time Sean lived on his own.

ANGEL: You can't control everyone's life.

GEORGE: I'm not trying to control his life.

ANGEL: What are you trying to do then ?

GEORGE: Get Sean somewhere to live.

ANGEL: You can't even find yourself somewhere decent to live.

GEORGE: Sorry ?

ANGEL: Your attitude is always wrong George.

GEORGE: My life has nothing to do with this meeting.

ANGEL: I'm not suggesting...

GEORGE: You should remember your own professional code before criticising me.

ANGEL: I'm not sure what you mean George.

GEORGE: It was good enough for you for one night ?

ANGEL: I will be taking this up with your line manager in the morning.

GEORGE: All of it ?

ANGEL: Fuck you George.

Angel leaves.

TEST: I'm not sure I followed that, but...

GEORGE: Most of it had nothing to do with you anyway.

TEST: But I do tend to agree with Miss Angel that it wasn't necessary to reveal that information to the general meeting.

GEORGE: She's married.

TEST: What's that got to do with it ?

GEORGE: Ask her husband.

TEST: About what ?

GEORGE: Anything you want ?

TEST: I fail to see what her marital status has to do with a clients meeting George ?

GEORGE: So you have an opinion on this ?

TEST: Of course.

GEORGE: And that's it ?

TEST: I do hope you're not trying to be insulting George.

GEORGE: No I'm not trying.

TEST: It's just that with the future of the Centre and the Service so uncertain I think it is time that we all worked together.

GEORGE: For what ?

TEST: Well there are certain things that we all believe in surely?

GEORGE: What do you believe in ?

TEST: I'm not sure what you mean George.

GEORGE: May I ask how the hell you got your job ?

TEST: It was a long time ago now.

GEORGE: Were you always this incompetant or did you work at it ?

TEST: How dare you speak to me like that.

GEORGE: They're just words Test.

TEST: You don't have any respect for anyone.

GEORGE: Yes I do. You watch me.

TEST: You've always been trouble George. Can't you see there are other peole here ?

GEORGE: You ?

TEST: — I'll need to speak to your line manager in the morning as well George.

GEORGE: Great you can all have a party in there.

SEAN'S VIGIL III.
The picture is clearly visible and the sound audible. Sean arrives to take his place in the light. The scene holds for ten seconds.

Scene VII
Angel's Office.

ANGEL: Hello Sean.

SEAN: I'm not late am I ? My father was late this morning. I didn't get ready. I'm not late though ?

ANGEL: No Sean. It's only two o'clock.

SEAN: 'Cause I wouldn't want to be late, George said I shouldn't be late for this. I should be on time. That's what he said. I'm always late. I can't seem to help it, I do my...

ANGEL: Sean, it's fine, please sit down.

SEAN: I'm never late for the papers though, George says we're always in time for them. I like that, being on time. When I'm not late.

ANGEL: Has your father told you why you're here Sean?

SEAN: Yes.

ANGEL: What did he say ?

251

SEAN: That I've got to be here and I've got to answer all the questions.

ANGEL: And he told you what we will be dicussing — talking about ?

SEAN: Oh yeh.

ANGEL: And ?

SEAN: Questions, I've got answer them.

ANGEL: We're here to talk about where you're going to live.

SEAN: It's okay, I'm back living with my Dad. Not at the hospital. Didn't like it there.

ANGEL: I know you didn't enjoy it there Sean, but it was only a short time wasn't it ?

SEAN: I like living with my Dad.

ANGEL: Your father has probably mentioned the chance of living more independently. Perhaps having your own place ?

SEAN: My Dad says I can always live with him if I want to.

ANGEL: Most people Sean when they're older they have to live alone.

SEAN: My Dad don't want to live alone.

ANGEL: Like your Sister, she lives alone.

SEAN: She lives with Uncle Michael, and my cousins. I'm their uncle. They call me Uncle Sean.

ANGEL: But your sister had to move away, perhaps not to live on her own but to live with someone else.

SEAN: I don't want to live on my own.

ANGEL: Perhaps not on your own but with a friend ?

SEAN: Like George ? George stayed at our house last night, perhaps I can live with him ?

ANGEL: Sean, your father thinks you might like to live with a friend.

SEAN: My mother told me I had to look after my Dad. She told me.

ANGEL: Sometimes the best way of looking after someone is to allow them to live on their own.

SEAN: What ?

ANGEL: And the best for you because now you're older you'll have to start doing more things for yourself.

SEAN: I do things for myself, now, honest.

ANGEL: There's a young man about your age, needs someone to live with him. He's got a spare room and we thought that you may like to meet him.

SEAN: Why would he want me to live with him ?

ANGEL: I think he's on his own and you can share the bills and things like that.

SEAN: What's bills ?

ANGEL: Money, you need to pay it, for things, to live.

SEAN: I don't pay any money.

ANGEL: When people earn money they have to use some of that money to pay for things like water and electricity.

SEAN: I earn money. I spend it at the weekend going to the cinema. I pay for Sarah sometimes.

ANGEL: Yes I understand that but now perhaps when you're living with someone, sharing a house, you might like to use some of that money to pay for food and things ?

SEAN: Yeh I might do that. If someone asked me.

ANGEL: This man, his name's Andy. Would you like to meet

him?

SEAN: Does he go to the centre ?

ANGEL: No.

SEAN: 'Cause I know Andy from the centre. Don't want to share with him.

ANGEL: No he's not at the centre.

SEAN: Good.

ANGEL: Would you like to meet him ?

SEAN: *(Sean shrugs)*

ANGEL: He lives near where you deliver papers.

SEAN: Do I give him a paper ?

ANGEL: I'm not sure.

SEAN: 'Cause if I do I could get the papers myself. And I wouldn't miss him out. Not when I knew him.

ANGEL: When you meet him perhaps you could ask him.

SEAN: Yeh, I'll do that.

ANGEL: So you'll come and meet Andy and think about living with him ?

SEAN: I can't leave my Dad. My mother said look after him.

ANGEL: Sean, sometimes, circumstances. They force people to do things they don't really want to. You'll like living with Andy. It'll be a change for you, think of it as a long holiday.

SEAN: I been on holiday. I didn't like it.

ANGEL: Your Dad can visit you.

SEAN: They said that about the hospital.

ANGEL: I'm sure he will this time.

SEAN: George said I wouldn't have to go back to the hospital.

ANGEL: I don't think you will...

SEAN: 'Cause I didn't like it there. Not a nice place.

ANGEL: If you move in with Andy you won't need to go back to the hospital.

SEAN: And I don't want to leave my Dad.

ANGEL: You won't need to leave him alone. You can visit him. On the weekends and things.

SEAN: I see Sarah on Saturdays.

ANGEL: You can see your father on a Sunday then.

SEAN: I can't leave my Dad, my Mam said.

ANGEL: If you don't move in with Andy now, he might find someone else and you might have to go back to the hospital.

SEAN: I, I...

Knock at door, George enters.

GEORGE: Ready ?

SEAN: George.

ANGEL: Yes we're ready.

GEORGE: I got the car out the back. Down to see Andy right Sean ?

SEAN: Right George.

GEORGE: You'll like Andy, he's a good lad. Lives in this great house where we deliver papers.

SEAN: Really George ?

GEORGE: Would I lie to you ?

SEAN: No of course not George.

GEORGE: Good. Go down and open the car Sean. We'll be right there. And hey, don't drive it away right ?

SEAN: I wouldn't do that George.

GEORGE: Go on.

Sean leaves.

GEORGE: How was it going ?

ANGEL: I was just explaining the necessity of the move to Sean.

GEORGE: How did you do ?

ANGEL: Fucking terrible.

GEORGE: That good aye.

ANGEL: I was just about to threaten him with shock treatment.

GEORGE: He looked a bit worked up ?

ANGEL: His mother made him promise to look after his father.

GEORGE: Hell, I was hoping he'd forgotten about that.

ANGEL: He's told you about it ?

GEORGE: When we first admitted him to the hospital.

ANGEL: Will he listen to you ?

GEORGE: When I tell him now, but he won't keep listening.

ANGEL: He seemed keen to meet Andy ?

GEORGE: I don't know how he'll react. He's not predictable. That's one of his problems.

ANGEL: But if it's that or...

GEORGE: Doesn't matter. He might agree to move in. Next week he's back at his Dad's with no memory of living anywhere else.

ANGEL: He stayed at the hospital.

GEORGE: It was a locked ward. He couldn't get out.

ANGEL: Great George, you came up with the bloody idea.

GEORGE: It'll work. Just need to be positive. That's what I need to be.

ANGEL: You'll need to be more than that George, you heard his sister.

GEORGE: There wasn't another option.

ANGEL: There isn't now.

GEORGE: If he likes Andy's and forgets about his bloody mother's promise he might stay.

ANGEL: It seemed lodged in there.

GEORGE: Sean's memory of what his mother said, maybe we can twist it a bit.

ANGEL: You can't do that ?

GEORGE: Why not ? What choice do I have ?

ANGEL: What happened to your sanctity of self-determination speech ?

GEORGE: Which draft did you read ?

ANGEL: George you're a bastard at times.

GEORGE: I get by.

ANGEL: Have you managed to speak to his father ?

GEORGE: Not yet.

ANGEL: But you were there last night.

GEORGE: How'd you know that ?

ANGEL: Sean told me.

GEORGE: Mr.Dent wasn't in a very talkative mood.

ANGEL: Why ?

GEORGE: Police picked him up outside the snooker club.

ANGEL: What for ?

GEORGE: Being unconscious.

ANGEL: Who told you ?

GEORGE: Neighbour rang me when he didn't return home.

ANGEL: You've been at his house all night?

GEORGE: Sure, he's got a better TV than me. There was a great film on at four, it was set in New York in the fifties, my era.

ANGEL: You're getting too involved again.

GEORGE: No, I'm not. This is me. I have to live like this.

ANGEL: There's only so much commitment you can give.

GEORGE: I've got enough for this one.

ANGEL: What if you leave George? What then ?

GEORGE: Maybe he'll have enough friends by then. A circle, other people to support him. I've read about this system in America, it's really working.

ANGEL: That's a different world.

GEORGE: And they've tried it in this country. Bristol I think.

ANGEL: It's just another new idea.

GEORGE: This one's different, you get people directly involved in his life. Friends who want to be there.

ANGEL: You know how hard it is to make friends.

GEORGE: This works, we just need to push it along.

ANGEL: Who's going to organise it ?

GEORGE: It works.

ANGEL: We're the only ones who're going to do it George. And because we're paid for it.

GEORGE: You're not just in it for the money Angel.

ANGEL: There's only so much. I have my own family. Other things.

GEORGE: There you are then.

ANGEL: Sorry I didn't mean it like that .

GEORGE: Don't worry about it. I know who I am.

ANGEL: Do you George ?

GEORGE: You don't know me Angel.
*
ANGEL: Don't give me that.

GEORGE: Why not ? I'm just the guy in the leather who doesn't give a damn. That's who you want to think George is.

ANGEL: What did I have to do ? Spend six months with you before I dare say anything ?

GEORGE: You only know me through this and one easy night.

ANGEL: This is your life.

GEORGE: Thanks a lot. I'm that hollow am I ?

ANGEL: You won't let anyone in will you ?

GEORGE: I've tried that.

ANGEL: And ?

GEORGE: Tears and promises.

ANGEL: You didn't try that with me. I could have been anyone.

GEORGE: Didn't need to. — That was me. You just couldn't see it.

ANGEL: I'm not who you think.

GEORGE: A respectable, married, career woman.

ANGEL: How respectable ?

GEORGE: I don't care anymore.

ANGEL: That's right dismiss it. It never happened.

GEORGE: It was just sex.

ANGEL: Exactly. You just keep living like this.

GEORGE: I will.

ANGEL: What do you want me to do ? Say sorry that I only wanted a night with you ?

GEORGE: See me Saturday ?

ANGEL: No.

GEORGE: Why ?

ANGEL: Steve is home this weekend.

GEORGE: Next week then ?

ANGEL: It's not going to happen George.

GEORGE: Nah you're right. It never fucking happened. — C'mon let's get out of here. This place.
**

* — ** Inclusive. Text added after first production.

VIGIL IV
Clear screen, sound in fragments.

Scene VIII
Training centre dining hall. Sarah & Sean.

SEAN: Is your mother taking us out this weekend ?

SARAH: I think so.

SEAN: Are you sure ?

SARAH: Yes.

SEAN: Really ?

SARAH: Why ?

SEAN: Because George is away.

SARAH: What's he away for ?

SEAN: Said he was going to London.

SARAH: Why's he going there ?

SEAN: Don't know, — he goes then comes back.

SARAH: Perhaps he knows someone ?

SEAN: Yeh, that must be it Sarah. He must know someone.

SARAH: I've been to London.

SEAN: You haven't ?

SARAH: Yeh my mother and father used to take me.

SEAN: Really ?

SARAH: Every year. I seen it all. All the sights. The palace and the other things.

SEAN: My father took me to Newport. That's a long way.

SARAH: Not as far as London.

SEAN: No, I don't think so. We went on the train though.

SARAH: My father used to live in London hospital.

SEAN: Why ?

SARAH: I don't know, he used to work there, in the hospital, in London.

SEAN: Does he still live there ?

SARAH: He lives in our house, with my mother. Why would he live in the hospital ?

SEAN: Have you ever been to the hospital ?

SARAH: Of course.

SEAN: What for ?

SARAH: 'Cause my father works there.

SEAN: I've been to the hospital.

SARAH: My father's hospital ?

SEAN: Don't know, don't know your father.

SARAH: He's tall, he's, —

SEAN: Might have seen him.

SARAH: He knows everyone in the hospital.

SEAN: I didn't like it.

SARAH: You'll like my father.

SEAN: Why ?

SARAH: 'Course you will, everyone likes my father. People call him Sir.

SEAN: Didn't like the hospital.

SARAH: You'll like him. He likes you.

SEAN: Does he ?

SARAH: I told him about you. He likes people who got a job.

SEAN: You told him about the papers ?

SARAH: My mother did. She said he likes to know things about people. Who they are, where they're from and things.

SEAN: Did he know people in London ?

SARAH: 'Course he did. He knew everyone there.

SEAN: Imagine knowing everyone. That would be great.

SARAH: Why ?

SEAN: Er, I could go and see them.

SARAH: You couldn't go to London.

SEAN: I could, I could go if I wanted.

SARAH: How ?

SEAN: I could catch a train, or a bus or something. I could catch a bus from the gardens. I always catch a bus from the gardens.

SARAH: Not to London.

SEAN: And I could pay with the money from the papers. I could pay with that. Then I could. On the bus.

SARAH: If you did that where would I go on Saturday ?

SEAN: I'm not going this Saturday, and if I did I'd take you with me.

SARAH: You'd take me ?

SEAN: Sure I'd take you. We could go with George. He wouldn't mind.

SARAH: Yeh, ask George.

SEAN: I bet George knows everyone in London as well.

SARAH: My mother wouldn't mind then. She likes George.

SEAN: Does she ?

SARAH: She says he's reliable. That's what she said.

SEAN: I'll ask him tonight after the papers.

SARAH: Where would we stay ?

SEAN: We'd come back with George.

SARAH: We couldn't do that. You always stay in London.

SEAN: I couldn't stay there, I'm living at Andy's.

SARAH: You don't stay at Andy's every night.

SEAN: I do, I pay Andy money, for my room. And we share everything else.

SARAH: You stayed at your father's last Saturday.

SEAN: That's different. I'm allowed to stay at Dad's. That's what my mother said.

SARAH: I bet George stays in London.

SEAN: No he doesn't, he comes back.

SARAH: Not the same day.

SEAN: How would you know?

SARAH: We always stayed in a hotel.

SEAN: *(Sean looks away)*

SARAH: Would you like to stay with me in an hotel ?

SEAN: And George?

SARAH: No just us, me and you ? We could stay together.

SEAN: What about George?

SARAH: You don't want George with you all the time do you ?

SEAN: Of course not.

SARAH: When he takes us to the lakes. You wouldn't want him all day would you ? Watching ?

SEAN: No way.

SARAH: We could have a room and a bed together.

SEAN: In London?

SARAH: My mother and father always had a room on their own.

SEAN: Really?

SARAH: The hotel was big, and there were hundreds of rooms. And maids and lifts and things.

SEAN: We could have a room.

SARAH: It'd cost money.

SEAN: I got money. I got thirty pounds. My Dad keeps it for me.

SARAH: That'll be enough.

SEAN: I got more than that.

SARAH: You'll ask George then?

SEAN: Yeh, no problem.

SARAH: You are working tonight ?

SEAN: Yeh I'm working, people like to get their papers on a Thursday.

SARAH: You ask him, we can go then.

SEAN: It be good that.

SARAH: You won't forget ?

SEAN: No I'll ask him after, in the park.

SARAH: Good. (*Smiles leans over, briefly kisses him.*)
I got to go now. Mrs.Wilson's class.

Looks around then kisses him again but longer. Sean looks around after she's gone; lights dim on dining table cafeteria,Sean leaves.

Scene IX:
George saunters over to the bench with his paper bag. Sitting on the bench he picks a paper out of his bag skims through it, looks over his shoulder to scan the park, throws the paper in the bin.

    Sean appears; smiling as he lopes up to the bench. Sits down next to George, smiling straight ahead. He waits patiently for George to speak, agonises over opening the conversation but finally plunges in.

SEAN: I've finished George.

GEORGE: 'Ave you ? How many have you got left ?

SEAN: None George.

GEORGE: None ?

SEAN: I delivered them all this time.

GEORGE: Good.

SEAN: And the ones I didn't deliver I put in the bin by the chip shop.

GEORGE: What you do that for ?

SEAN: You do that don't you George ?

GEORGE: I know that but-- it's just that.

SEAN: That's okay innit ?

GEORGE: Never mind you've delivered them now.

George stares out, Sean looks around.

GEORGE: How are you getting on at Andy's ?

SEAN: I like it George, it's nice there, and I've got a room of my own.

GEORGE: How long is it now ?

SEAN: Three months.

GEORGE: Goes quick doesn't it ?

SEAN: I put posters up this week.

GEORGE: Yeh ?

SEAN: My father gave them to me.

GEORGE: Aye.

SEAN: He came around to see me he did. — On his own.

GEORGE: Good.

SEAN: I won't have to go back to the hospital now will I ?

GEORGE: I shouldn't think so.

SEAN: I don't want to go back there again. Not unless I have to.

GEORGE: It'll be fine as long as you keep looking after Andrew.

SEAN: I will George. Me and Andy are mates.

GEORGE: He's a good lad Andrew.

SEAN: Why can't he speak George ?

GEORGE: It's just one of those things. Some people just can't.

SEAN: He's older than me.

GEORGE: Aye, a good few years.

SEAN: He had a birthday party last week. That's when my Dad came to see me. Bethan was there. And Mrs.Angel came.

GEORGE: House-full.

SEAN: Why didn't you come George ?

GEORGE: Couldn't make it Wednesday.

SEAN: Andy had a cake with candles.

GEORGE: How old was he ?

SEAN: Thirty-four George.

GEORGE: You had a good time then ?

SEAN: Andy enjoyed it. He smiles all the time, so I know he likes me.

GEORGE: He's happy I guess.

SEAN: That's what it must be, cause he's always smiling. – Andrew hasn't got a mother either has he George ?

GEORGE: No, not anymore.

SEAN: I wish my Mam didn't have to go away though George.

GEORGE: I know you do Sean. Things just happen sometimes, can't do anything about them.

SEAN: Dad says she's in heaven now and if I'm good I can join her one day, that's right isn't it George ?

GEORGE: It might be Sean, but you'll be good anyway won't you ?

SEAN: Yes George.

GEORGE: But not too good aye ?

SEAN: No, not too good George.

SEAN: Where's heaven George ?

GEORGE: — I don't know Sean, but I'm sure your mother will be happy there.

SEAN: I wish she didn't have to go there though George, Dad says I can't even visit her or anything, not like when she was in hospital, I could visit her then.

GEORGE: How is Sarah ?

SEAN: She's great George, her mother's taking us to the pictures this weekend.

GEORGE: That's good, what are you going to see ?

SEAN: I don't know George, her mother's going to pick one for us.

GEORGE: I'm sure you'll enjoy it.

SEAN: Yes I will. It's dark and we can kiss in the cinema.

GEORGE: Don't you watch the film ?

SEAN: Yeh George we do, but Sarah likes kissing.

GEORGE: I'm sure she does.

SEAN: I like kissing George.

GEORGE: It's good fun Sean, most people like kissing.

SEAN: We do other things as well George.

GEORGE: In the cinema ?

SEAN: No, not there George.

GEORGE: What do you do Sean ?

SEAN: You know, kiss and...

GEORGE: Yeh and ?

SEAN: And kiss — I don't know.

GEORGE: You and Sarah, you happy Sean ?

SEAN: Yeh. She likes kissing George.

GEORGE: Good, any problems, anything bothering you, ask me right ?

George begins to fold papers.

SEAN: You know when you go to London, do you stay there?

GEORGE: Yeh of course.

SEAN: All night?

GEORGE: Sometimes.

SEAN: Why do you do that ?

GEORGE: Friends, I stay with friends.

SEAN: Could we come with you ? Me and Sarah ?

GEORGE: Why would you want to come with me? Don't you

see enough of me in the week?

SEAN: Course we do George. But we could stay in an hotel with a bed.

GEORGE: I don't stay in an hotel. I couldn't afford it.

SEAN: I can George, I got money.

GEORGE: You don't stay in an hotel, it's too expensive.

SEAN: Me and Sarah will.

GEORGE: There's plenty to do here without going to London.

SEAN: Don't you want us to come with you?

GEORGE: It's not that.

SEAN: I want to stay in an hotel with a bed.

GEORGE: Perhaps you can come with me later in the year. A day-trip or something.

SEAN: Sex is good isn't it George ?

GEORGE: Yes it's good, with the right person. (*To himself.*) Well it's pretty good with anybody really.

SEAN: What do you mean George ?

GEORGE: Nothing Sean. It's sex, it needs to be with someone special, someone you know really well.

SEAN: I know her really well.

GEORGE: Yeh course you do.

SEAN: You wouldn't do it with someone you didn't know well would you George ?

GEORGE: It just needs to be special that's all.

SEAN: It is George.

GEORGE: 'Course it is, ---look have you got, you know condoms and all that ?

SEAN: 'Course I have. Don't be daft. Condoms. Sorted all that no problem.

There is a short silence.

GEORGE: You haven't told anyone else about this have you Sean ?

SEAN: No way George, I wouldn't tell anyone else.

GEORGE: Well promise you won't tell anyone yet, especially her mother, alright ?

SEAN: Don't be stupid George I wouldn't do that.

GEORGE: Good. 'Course you wouldn't right ? What the hell am I on about right ? You're a working man.

SEAN: What do you mean George ?

GEORGE: Nothing mate. C'mon let's get going then or Andy will be thinking we've deserted him.

They both get up from the bench; George dumps his remaining papers into the bin. They walk out of the park.
The lights dim on the bench and rise on the desk.

Scene X:

Test arrives in the room. He is obviously in a panic and nervous. He fiddles ineffectually with files and papers on the desk before giving up and retreating to his chair at the far side. The office door is thrown open by George who arrives in a confusion of anger. He stands facing Test his hands spread rigidly upon the desk.

GEORGE: What happened ?

TEST: Sean has absconded.

GEORGE: Yeh, any particular reason?

TEST: It's a bit delicate George.

GEORGE: Delicate ?

TEST: We've had a bit of an unfortunate incident.

GEORGE: Concerning Sean ?

TEST: And Sarah Evans.

GEORGE: Are they okay ?

TEST: Yes fine, we think, at least Sarah is. She's at home. As I said we can't find Sean.

GEORGE: I thought he'd finished with all that. What the fuck happened?

TEST: Calm down George.

GEORGE: You tell me what happened then ?

TEST: You're aware that Sean and Sarah have been having what may be tacitly termed a relationship.

GEORGE: Yes I know that, I've been taking them out on the weekends.

TEST: Yes well, the relationship has developed further than we anticipated.

GEORGE: What do you mean, further than you anticipated ?

TEST: I was under the impression that it was to be conducted on a purely platonic level.

GEORGE: And who gave you that assurance ?

TEST: You did.

GEORGE: Rubbish.

TEST: You implied it.

GEORGE: You took what you wanted.

TEST: Anyway that's irrelevant now, they have developed a close personal relationship.

GEORGE: I was aware of that, so ?

TEST: You knew and you didn't inform us?

GEORGE: What the hell has it got to do with you ?

TEST: I am responsible for Sean Dent's and Sarah Evans' personal safety.

GEORGE: Not their bloody sex life.

TEST: They're not supposed to have a sex life.

GEORGE: Says who ?

TEST: Sarah's mother for one.

GEORGE: Fuck, you haven't told her ?

TEST: It was my obligation.

GEORGE: Bollocks.

TEST: For Christ sake George she's not even sterilised.

GEORGE: You bastard.

TEST: I find your attitude very unhelpful George, I would have expected more support from you in this delicate situation.

GEORGE: Support, I expect Sean and Sarah could have done with some support if not discretion, but no they get you exposing them like some fucking journalist.

TEST: For your information they were exposed, as you put it, by Mr. Watts in the pottery room and he's made an official complaint.

GEORGE: An official complaint. What the fuck for ? I suppose they messed up his precious clay.

TEST: Apparently Sean struck him.

GEORGE: Wouldn't you if Watts pulled you off the top of your Mrs. on a Sunday night ?

TEST: Judith has got nothing to do with this.

GEORGE: And neither has bloody Watts. (*Drops his voice as if addressing himself.*) A bit of life that's all he wanted and he was hanging onto it. —

TEST: I'm afraid we are going to have to suspend Sean for a week.

GEORGE: Don't tell me, unsuitable behaviour.

TEST: Will you be able to explain the situation to him ?

GEORGE: If I can find him.

TEST: It'll only be for a week or so George, just for appearances. The other clients...

GEORGE: Unsuitable behaviour, where else are they supposed to do it ?

TEST: It's not as simple as that.

GEORGE: He hasn't got a car, they can't stay at Andy's house on their own. Where are they supposed to do it ?

TEST: According to Mrs.Evans they're not supposed to do it at all.

GEORGE: Oh for fuck sake mun, you ever tried stopping ?

TEST: George I sympathise with what you're trying to do for Sean but you must appreciate the situation. The realities.

GEORGE: Sure I do.

TEST: He's an adult but he's not in control.

GEORGE: He hasn't got rights, go on, tell me.

TEST: You know the situation as well as I do George. It's not so easy anymore.

GEORGE: It's never going to be easy.

TEST: When I first joined the service...

GEORGE: Don't give me that. I've heard it before.

TEST: You don't listen to anyone else. Unless it's in a book you're not interested.

GEORGE: Yes I do, I listen to Sean.

TEST: And where's that got you ? Did you think this out ?

GEORGE: I was getting there.

TEST: It's a bit late now.

GEORGE: Easy for you to say. What the hell have you been doing for the last twenty years ? Look at the fucking place, falling down.

TEST: It's been my life too George.

GEORGE: And you settled for it.

TEST: I knew what I could do.

GEORGE: So you haven't risked anything have you ?

TEST: No, I've stayed together.

GEORGE: Leave me out of it.

TEST: You need to hold back.

GEORGE: He was doing alright for himself. —

TEST: Maybe you'll be able to talk to Sarah's mother ?

GEORGE: Yeh, maybe. — You've no idea where he ran to ?

TEST: He was heading into town.

GEORGE: Great.

TEST: Watts couldn't hold him. Apparently he was shouting something about going to London. Does that mean anything to you ?

GEORGE: He'll be at the Gardens.

TEST: What'll he be doing there?

GEORGE: He'll be waiting to catch a bus to London.

TEST: You can't catch a bus from there to London.
They go from the station.

GEORGE: *(George stares at Test.)*

TEST: What ?

GEORGE: Never mind. — And Sarah's okay?

TEST: Her mother picked her up.

GEORGE: Right I'll get down to the Gardens.

TEST: Shall I contact his father ?

GEORGE: Not worth it. Where's Watts ?

TEST: Gone home sick.

GEORGE: Lucky that.

TEST: There's no need for that George.

GEORGE: There was no need for any of it.

SEAN'S VIGIL V
The screen is tuned to the static. There is some sound but it is disjointed in form and volume. Sean watches the screen.

Scene XI
Sarah sits alone at the dressing table. Draws hard red marks across her perfect make-up with lipstick. Hands shaking. Mother arrives at doorway. She pushes the objects from her table onto the floor. Gets up, runs to her mother.

MRS.EVANS: It's alright. —
You haven't done anything wrong.
It's alright, don't worry. I'll speak to Dad.

SEAN'S VIGIL VI
Short rise and fall of the Vigil IV. The sound fading.
The screen is tuned to the static. There is some sound but it is disjointed in form and volume. Sean watches the screen.

Scene XII
The lake-side cafe. George is sitting alone at a table staring out. The edges to his life are showing. Waiting. Mrs.Evans arrives, she is elegant and composed. George half stands to greet her.

MRS.EVANS: Sorry I'm late.

GEORGE: Just here myself. Coffee ?

MRS.EVANS: No thank you.

GEORGE: I'm glad you agreed to come.

MRS.EVANS: Yes. I thought it best.

GEORGE: Well thanks all the same. — Sarah ?

MRS.EVANS: With my husband.

GEORGE: She's not too upset ?

MRS.EVANS: It was a very traumatic experience for her.

GEORGE: Of course.

MRS.EVANS: She's upset. But perhaps she'll be alright. She's quite a practical girl despite everything.

GEORGE: Yes very confident when we're out, more than Sean even, almost er.

MRS.EVANS: Normal ?

GEORGE: Not what I was going to say but — sorry.

MRS.EVANS: It's okay, that's what I think. A few more seconds of air and it would have been alright. I wouldn't need to deal with any of this. It would be just the easy things.

GEORGE: You can't think like that.

MRS.EVANS: Why not ? You do anyway.

GEORGE: She seems a happy girl.

MRS.EVANS: We do our best Mr.Rees.

GEORGE: I'm not doing this very well. I just thought I should speak to you, explain things.

MRS.EVANS: How are you going to do that ?

GEORGE: Try anyway. —

MRS.EVANS: I suppose you think I'm old fashioned interfering?

GEORGE: No, not at all.

MRS.EVANS: No matter, I should have been expecting it really, she's old enough easily, but she's still young.

GEORGE: Perhaps they all seem that to us ?

MRS.EVANS: Yes maybe, perhaps she would have seemed young however old she was, but. — But I have to make that decision for her now. She doesn't see all the possibilities as I'm sure you're aware.

GEORGE: Sean asked about condoms, he knows enough that way.

MRS.EVANS: So you knew about it ?

GEORGE: He mentioned something, but — its hard to know how much ...

MRS.EVANS: And you think he knows enough ?

GEORGE: I was working my way through it.

MRS.EVANS: And how long would that have taken you ?

GEORGE: He only just mentioned ...

MRS.EVANS: They've been seeing each other four months.

GEORGE: Yes but he ...

MRS.EVANS: Something could have easily gone wrong ?

GEORGE: I know that but they had ...

MRS.EVANS: Do you Mr.Rees? Do you really know what could have gone wrong?

GEORGE: It's always a risk, whoever you are.

MRS.EVANS: But you weren't at risk.

GEORGE: No.

MRS.EVANS: You don't see it do you ?

GEORGE: Yes I do. I just can't think of them as anything but two young people.

MRS.EVANS: I don't think Sean was taking advantage of her Mr.Rees.

GEORGE: He wasn't I'm sure.

MRS.EVANS: You were supposed to be taking them to London.

GEORGE: I never said that. Sean asked but I couldn't have done that.

MRS.EVANS: Not without speaking to me ?

GEORGE: It was just one of his ideas.

MRS.EVANS: Sarah asked me about London too. So maybe I didn't want to listen to what she was saying either.

GEORGE: I was listening. I always listen to people.

MRS.EVANS: You don't understand. I want her to enjoy herself. It's just I haven't had a chance to explain it all, there's so much to it. Sarah can have her life, it's — only natural. Although I'm going to have a hell of a time explaining that to Richard. He doesn't really want her to grow up.

GEORGE: But she has.

MRS.EVANS: He won't see it that way.

GEORGE: He's a doctor.

MRS.EVANS: So what ?

GEORGE: I just thought he would have seen other things, other people ?

MRS.EVANS: Yes of course he has but this isn't other people.

GEORGE: No.

MRS.EVANS: It's not Richard I'm worried about. If she gets pregnant, what then ? Who's going to bring up the child ? Me again ? I couldn't, not again. And Sarah ? She's not up to that, she's capable but not for that.

GEORGE: She'd get support. Care homes ?

MRS.EVANS: You can't believe that ?

GEORGE: Sometimes.

MRS.EVANS: I know you've got Sean's best interests at heart and probably Sarah's but you only work with him, you're a friend, we're family. Friends lose touch. But we can't, we've always got to be there.

GEORGE: They could move in together somewhere, get a council house, share a life. I've been reading about it. It could work.

MRS.EVANS: They're children underneath Mr.Rees.

GEORGE: No they're not, they can't be. They're different that's all.

MRS.EVANS: Is that what you really think ?

GEORGE: They could live together.

MRS.EVANS: Why are you so involved ?

GEORGE: He's my friend. I have to be.

MRS.EVANS: What else ?

GEORGE: Nothing it's just me.

MRS.EVANS: Perhaps you're right. — You're a romantic like that aren't you ?

GEORGE: It has happened before. I've read about it. I'll convince them.

MRS.EVANS: That's not so easy, convincing people.

GEORGE: I'm good at it.

MRS.EVANS: The council hope we'll take care of her, then when we die they'll pick up the remainder and you know what? They're right, we'll probably do that.

GEORGE: With a house maybe they'll be OK. There'll be other people around, help them make decisions.

MRS.EVANS: Would you like that ? Someone making your life, not family but half–friends, employees ?

GEORGE: Dunno. Maybe I could use more support.

MRS.EVANS: Not married ?

GEORGE: Not anymore.

MRS.EVANS: I'm sorry.

GEORGE: Don't be, she's better off without me. — I drift. And when I don't drift I drink.

MRS.EVANS: (*She leans across the table to hold his hands.*) They'll be alright Mr.Rees. I can cope with it.

SEAN'S VIGIL VII
The screen is tuned to the twilight zone between the picture and the static. The sound breaks through in pieces.

Scene XIII:
Jazz club. Saturday.
George wanders in with two pint glasses in his hands. He calls Sean to join him. A club regular sits at a table, waiting for the music.

GEORGE: Here we are, this will do.
(They sit silently at first; George scans the room for points of interest, Sean considers the prospects of his beer.)
You wanted to come out tonight didn't you ?

SEAN: Yes George.

GEORGE: It's better to get out, the music will take your mind off things. —
It's over for, now try to forget about it.

SEAN: Is this a pub George ?

GEORGE: Yeh sort of pub club.

SEAN: Are they going to play music here George ?

GEORGE: 'Course they are.

SEAN: Not many people in here though George ?

GEORGE: It'll fill up, there's a good night here, you'll enjoy it.

SEAN: Not many people here though.

GEORGE: But we're here, me and you.

SEAN: Usually go to the cinema on a Saturday.

GEORGE: Yeh I know that but...

SEAN: Sarah's mum picks the film for us. I pay though George. I got money. Do you want a drink George ?

GEORGE: I'm fine with this one for now Sean.

SEAN: We didn't do anything wrong did we George ?

GEORGE: No.

SEAN: Sarah still goes to the centre don't she ? Every day. Then on the weekend we go out. Next weekend George ?

GEORGE: We'll have to see how things work out.

SEAN: You said it was good didn't you George, and everybody does it don't they ?

GEORGE: Some people don't like to be reminded of it that's all.

SEAN: I'll be able to see Sarah again won't I ?

George hesitates before answering.

GEORGE: Sure, you'll be back at the centre in a week.

SEAN: Will I be able to take her out next weekend ?

GEORGE: We'll have to see what her mother says, you know she's not happy with you at the moment.

Sean smiles in embarrassment at George who tries to banish a smile from his face but can't. Sean smiles more assuredly back before returning to stare at his pint.

SEAN: Sarah's alright though George ?

GEORGE: Yeh don't worry she's fine.

SEAN: I want to be able to see her George, I don't want it to be like Mum, I don't want her to go to heaven.

GEORGE: No it's not like that, it's just that you've split up for a while that's all, lots of people split up.

SEAN: I don't want to split up though George.

GEORGE: I know that, sometimes it just happens that's all, — Here we are mun.

Indicates the performer who they follow with their eyes; there is a burst of clapping following his arrival which is enthusiastically chorused by Sean.

SEAN: What's he going to play George ?

GEORGE: He's going to be playing some jazz.

They wait on the performer.

SEAN: What's jazz George ?

GEORGE: It's, — well he sort of gets up there and plays what he wants to think, he follows the rhythms.

SEAN: Will he be like the Stones ?

GEORGE: Not exactly like the Stones, I don't think he'll be singing.

SEAN: I like the Stones, my Dad used to buy me all the records. I used to have a record every Christmas. Do you think he'll get me one this Christmas?

GEORGE: He might, — no I'm sure he will, what's the latest album ?

SEAN: I don't know George.

GEORGE: I'm sure he'll know.

SEAN: He bought me a poster.

GEORGE: Have a drink Sean. Got to keep quiet when he's playing.

SEAN: (*Nods, then drinks.*) He always gets me the right album, I used to like The Police as well, but you can't get them anymore can you George ?

GEORGE: No they've split up.

SEAN: Like me and Sarah ?

GEORGE: A bit like that.

Sean appears satisfied by this answer and turns his attention to the guitarist who has been playing; but he soon re-embarks on an attempted conversation. The man in front turns briefly around to see who is talking.

SEAN: Why isn't he going to sing then George ?

GEORGE: They don't in Jazz Sean.

SEAN: I like singing George. — Why is he closing his eyes George ?

GEORGE: I'm not sure, we'll talk about it later.

SEAN: Sure George, we'll talk about it later, I couldn't play with my eyes closed though, I wouldn't be able to see. I can play you know George ?

George bows his head uneasily; man in front turns around and directs his speech sharply at Sean.

MAN: Look mate I didn't pay two fifty to hear you ramble on about your guitar playing. (*Holds a stare then turns away.*)

SEAN: Why did he say that George ?

GEORGE: Ignore him Sean.

SEAN: But I was only talking.

MAN: Can't you shut him up ?

GEORGE: No.

MAN: Dunno why you bring people like that in here.

GEORGE: Like what ?

MAN: Like him.

GEORGE: That so. And you're an expert ?

MAN: I'm trying to listen to this music.

GEORGE: Why don't you try an' do that then ?

MAN: You think you'd have some consideration for others.

Sean, visibly upset, turns to George. George puts a finger to his lips to indicate silence, then to get up and make their way to the exit.

SEAN: Why was he saying that George ?

GEORGE: Some people are just like that Sean.

SEAN: I was only talking.

GEORGE: I know, don't worry about it,

SEAN: But George I...

GEORGE: Look Sean I want you to do me a favour right, here's a fiver. You go out on the street and get a taxi home. I'll catch another one in a while. Can you do that for me ?

SEAN: I don't want to go home yet George.

GEORGE: I know that, but we have to. I'll write the address down just in case you forget it right ? Just give this to the taxi driver and he'll get you home. Tell Bethan I had to stay out alright ? — You clear what you're going to do ?

SEAN: I'm enjoying myself really George. Don't send me home like my Dad. I don' t want to go yet.

GEORGE: I just need you to do this for me, okay.

SEAN: *(Sean nods.)*

GEORGE: You clear what you got to do ?

SEAN: *(Sean nods.)*

GEORGE: There'll be plenty of taxis, you just catch one home.

Sean leaves.George re-enters the bar, checks his pocket for change and isolates three coins. He walks up to the man who looks up as George dumps the coins into his pint.

GEORGE: Here's your fucking two fifty mate.

MAN: *(Stands up sharply.)* You bastard...

George sizes up into the classic boxing pose. The laughter of earlier vigil scene cuts the light into darkness.

VIGIL SCENE VIII
Twilight zone.
Sound more audible, screen begins to clear.

Scene XIV
Collins' newspaper shop off the Corporation Road.
Dead end of November.
Collins is alone counting figures on a calculator.
Door opens to Sean.

COLLINS: Sean ?

SEAN: Come for my papers Mr.Collins.

COLLINS: Where's George ?

SEAN: *(Shrugs.)*

COLLINS: Thought you had given it up ?

SEAN: Not me Mr.Collins, I'm here.

COLLINS: Where were you last week ?

SEAN: I was ill Mr.Collins

COLLINS: Really ?

SEAN: Very ill Mr.Collins.

COLLINS: And George ?

SEAN: Dunno.

COLLINS: Someone rang about George — he's given it up and you can't do it without him.

SEAN: Not me Mr.Collins. I'm here.

COLLINS: On your own ?

SEAN: I know the houses, honest I do Mr.Collins. The Embankment and the flats.

COLLINS: Well I'm not sure, all these papers...

SEAN: Please Mr.Collins I got to do it.

COLLINS: Need the money do you son ?

SEAN: (*Nods.*)

COLLINS: Got a girl have you ?

SEAN: Yes Mr.Collins.

COLLINS: Expensive things, son.

SEAN: She pays sometimes Mr.Collins

COLLINS: Got a good one there then.

SEAN: Or her mother does.

COLLINS: Even better.

SEAN: I'm saving Mr.Collins.

COLLINS: What for ?

SEAN: We're going to London.

COLLINS: Bloody waste of money that son, I can tell you.

SEAN: And other things.

COLLINS: Yeh I'm sure. Ah what the hell, you want it you can do it.

SEAN: I'll do it right Mr.Collins.

COLLINS: How many papers you usually take ?

SEAN: Er, papers, George usually does the numbers Mr.Collins but...

COLLINS: How many streets is it ?

SEAN: It's the Embankment and the Gardens.

COLLINS: That's thirty nine the Embankment, twelve for the Gardens, nine for the close. And the flats take twelve. That's er...

SEAN: That's .... It's ......

COLLINS: Here's hundred. (*Hands him a tied bundle.*) That should cover it.

SEAN: Right Mr.Collins, I'll do it right through, all the houses.

COLLINS: Yes I'm sure. (*Pushes a stack of papers across to him. Sean begins to place them into his bag.*)

SEAN: Got them Mr.Collins.

COLLINS: What you waiting for then ?

SEAN: Nothing, I'm going to do them. Thanks Mr.Collins.

VIGIL SCENE IX
Short rise and fall of clear screen.
The Rolling Stones 'Can't Always Get What You Want'.
'Gimme Shelter' used in other parts.

End

The additional two scenes have been written since the first production and could form part of a re-structured version of the play in a future production.

Scene A
Sean's House. George sitting alone half-sleeping half reading. He holds a huge volume of the Collected Writings of Karl Marx. Grigeli enters. Looks over at George.

GRIGELI: Morning.

GEORGE: — Oh hello love.

GRIGELI: Didn't know Dad was taking in lodgers ?

GEORGE: I just called in. Did you get my message ?

GRIGELI: What ?

GEORGE: I rang your house, spoke to your husband.

GRIGELI: He was up was he ?

GEORGE: He is now.

GRIGELI: I haven't been home yet.

GEORGE: Just finished your shift ?

GRIGELI: Yeh. I usually call into see Dad. He's not at his best right now.

GEORGE: I don't think he'll be that bright this morning.

GRIGELI: Drunk ?

GEORGE: Aye.

GRIGELI: — How did you get in ?

GEORGE: Philips, next door.

GRIGELI: He rang you did he ?

GEORGE: He was worried about Sean when your Dad didn't make it home.

GRIGELI: Is Sean alright ?

GEORGE: I think he missed his medication.

GRIGELI: Shit. Dad shouldn't forget about that. He knows he needs it.

GEORGE: Found him in front of the TV.

GRIGELI: He had a fit ?

GEORGE: I think so.

GRIGELI: Shit. He can't stay here. You've got to get him some care.

GEORGE: I'm working on it.

GRIGELI: I'll look after him Dad said. I'll not have him stay another night in that hospital. How long did that last ? Straight down the Langrove for another skinful.

GEORGE: We've got a meeting at the house today. It might go through in a week.

GRIGELI: Should have left him in the hospital.

GEORGE: He hated it.

GRIGELI: So what ? Do you think I like working ten hour shifts while that useless bastard husband of mine can't get off his arse to find a job?

GEORGE: — I'll get Sean a place in this house. Another week.

GRIGELI: That woman rang me. Wanted us all to go down and meet Andy what's his bloody name's carers. Told her I couldn't make it because I was working. Suggested I could ask for some time off on compassionate grounds. You can tell she's never worked for Coates Soft Drinks and Orange. You know what the perk of my job is ? After a ten hour shift they give you a carton of juice. Something to take home for the kids. Ask her if she'd work a night shift for a bloody soft drink.

GEORGE: Angel tries hard. Sometimes she's a bit too focused if you know what I mean ?

GRIGELI: Is that the same as saying she doesn't live in the real world ?

GEORGE: No that's my problem.

GRIGELI: — My mother used to think the world of you. — Can't think why.

GEORGE: I have my plus points.

GRIGELI: Well hidden are they ?

GEORGE: Very.

GRIGELI: You've been in hospital haven't you ?

GEORGE: Don't hold back the questions like. Don't spare my feelings.

GRIGELI: Just something to say.

GEORGE: Aye, used to get stitched up after every fight.

GRIGELI: The type of hospital when they won't let you out ?

GEORGE: No.

GRIGELI: Is that why you want to help Sean ?

GEORGE: It's nothing to do with that. He just needs a bit of guidance. He's alright Sean. He's almost there.

GRIGELI: My mother told me about it. Think that's why she liked you. A gentleman she used to say. A hurt, gentle, man.

GEORGE: She obviously hadn't seen me box. Pure violence I was.

GRIGELI: She knew you well enough.

GEORGE: Everyone thinks they fucking know me. Couple more conversations and you'll have an opinion.

GRIGELI: I have that already.

GEORGE: Aye I'm sure.

GRIGELI: Don't get touchy. Only asking. — Sean up yet ?

GEORGE: Sleeping it off.

GRIGELI: Was he conscious when you found him ?

GEORGE: Out of it. But I think he was sleeping by then. Difficult to wake him when he's like that.

GRIGELI: Fucking dangerous to wake him.

GEORGE: I think he must have smashed the lamp when he fell over.

GRIGELI: Never liked it anyway.

GEORGE: He had a couple of scratches on his face.

GRIGELI: He does that when he's fitting sometimes. — How did you get him to bed ?

GEORGE: Carried him.

GRIGELI: And Dad ?

GEORGE: The police carried him.

GRIGELI: Not again. They charge him ?

GEORGE: Apparently not. I think the Copper knew him.

GRIGELI: Did he have red hair ? Big ?

GEORGE: That's the one.

GRIGELI: Christopher Parry, he used to live on the bottom of the road. Couple of years older than Sean, liked to think he was his big brother. Chris got into so many fights over him. Stupid things like names but he wouldn't let anything go, no matter how big they were.

GEORGE: Looked like he could handle himself.

GRIGELI: He could do that.

GEORGE: Knew him well then ?

GRIGELI: Now who's asking the questions ?

GEORGE: That's my job. Looking after people you need to know who they are. Now your father, he could do with some more support.

GRIGELI: What about AA. That would appeal to your little friend at the office.Would it be possible to discuss the problems with your father ? Talk about what he needs in terms of support. Do you think you father would benefit from some counselling at this time ? I'll give her bloody counselling.

GEORGE: It's the language that get's you.

GRIGELI: It is not just the bloody language. It's that she doesn't really care.

GEORGE: She does. She just comes across cold.

GRIGELI: Slept with her have you ?

GEORGE: Fuck mun, it's seven o'clock in the morning.

GRIGELI: So ?

GEORGE: What's it got to do with you ?

GRIGELI: Thought you had.

GEORGE: No.

GRIGELI: Liar.

GEORGE: Why should I ?

GRIGELI: And I bet she's married.

GEORGE: Has anyone ever accused you of being blunt ?

GRIGELI: Tactful I am. Like my mother.

GEORGE: I'd noticed.

GRIGELI: Better than talking about the weather.

GEORGE: Yeh — I'll go and get Sean.

Grigeli has been getting closer to George. She now kisses him.

GEORGE: What you do that for ?

GRIGELI: Wanted to see what you would do ?

GEORGE: And ?

GRIGELI: Just as I thought.

GEORGE: So ?

GRIGELI: It's an empty house and I've just finished ten hours.

GEORGE: I'll go and check on Sean.

GRIGELI: No you won't.

Kisses him. Lights fade.

Scene B
Angel's House. Late evening/early morning. Angel moves to answer the door. She pulls away as George enters.

ANGEL: It's late.

GEORGE: Yeh. Couldn't make it earlier.

ANGEL: Your face ? (*Brushes blood away.*)

GEORGE: Slight diffrence of opinion.

ANGEL: Over what ?

GEORGE: Music.

ANGEL: And you end up with a broken nose.

GEORGE: He was a free-form man, me I'm more into rhythm with vocals. You know the type, argue over anything.

ANGEL: Had you been drinking ?

GEORGE: No funny enough I hadn't. It was an intellectual discussion, — that got out of hand.

ANGEL: — You shouldn't have come here.

GEORGE: I was passing, thought I'd call in.

ANGEL: At three o'clock in the morning ?

GEORGE: I always walk at this hour, clears the mind.

ANGEL: What if Steve was here ?

GEORGE: He's not.

ANGEL: You didn't know that.

GEORGE: I checked with his firm.

ANGEL: You, — infuriate me. I've told you it's not going to happen between us.

GEORGE: And I'm saying it is.

ANGEL: I'm married George.

GEORGE: You don't love him.

ANGEL: That's none of your business.

GEORGE: There's not many chances at this Angel.

ANGEL: You don't understand me do you ? I don't want your life.

GEORGE: Are you going to leave him ?

ANGEL: — Yes.

GEORGE: Come with me.

ANGEL: Where ? To that tiny little flat ?

GEORGE: I've told you before, leave my house out of it.

ANGEL: I couldn't live with you. I've just realised I can't live with him.

GEORGE: I'm leaving it Angel, come with me.

ANGEL: No.

GEORGE: Out of this city.

ANGEL: What you going to do ?

GEORGE: I don't know yet. Sell flowers ? People must be happy when they buy flowers.

ANGEL: For funerals ?

GEORGE: I've thought about that. I'll have a street stall. You don't buy funeral flowers from the street.

ANGEL: Where are you going to go ?

GEORGE: Back to London.

ANGEL: You hated it.

GEORGE: It had its good parts.

ANGEL: Not where you'll be living.

GEORGE: I'll get a better flat, Housing Association, somewhere down in Battersea, close to the market. We'd be alright there. Sean and Sarah can come and visit. They can have a room with a bed. Yeh that's the answer.

ANGEL: You aren't blaming yourself for that ?

GEORGE: 'Course I am. I should have listened to him.

ANGEL: I heard Mrs.Evans was more reasonable than you expected.

GEORGE: Bloody *Guardian* reader. I had her down as a reactionary. More real than the lot of us. She'll be taking the both of them to sex education classes next.

ANGEL: You were too close to him.

GEORGE: Not after tonight.

ANGEL: You didn't fight with him ?

GEORGE: C'mon — ?

ANGEL: Stupid question. — It's late George.

GEORGE: And ?

ANGEL: You've got to go.

GEORGE: No I haven't.

ANGEL: It was one of those things, it just happened.

GEORGE: I know that. I just want, — more.

ANGEL: There isn't anymore.

GEORGE: Tonight. I'm going then.

ANGEL: — It's not easy.
Draws him into her. They kiss.

James Westaway, Dorien Thomas   *photo: L.D.*

Lowri Mae, Sharon Morgan, James Westaway,
David Middleton, Dorien Thomas

photo: L.D.

New Welsh Drama

AND THIS FROM ME IS MY VIEW

Ten years on and I still don't know. I guess what I do know is something about the intangible magic and truth of theatre and the telling of stories.

Lowri Mae

New writing from an actor's perspective. Now there's a large canvas. Trust me, the perspective isn't as narrow as you might think.

I'd never beg to play Hamlet. What's the point? I can't imagine that there's a single aspect I could bring to that role that hasn't been explored by someone else at some point in the play's long and illustrious history. Maybe the combination of line interpretations would be novel, but where's the jazz in that?

Creating something afresh, now that's where the pioneering is. It's exciting to rehearse a new play because you can't crib, you can't watch the film version, and you can't make decisions simply on the basis of bucking previous interpretations. There aren't any. You lock yourself away with a few other people and thrash out what makes the characters tick, and whether it works or not depends entirely on that group of people.

And there's the fun knowing that the first gig is yours, it will always be yours, it's owned by you. You blazed that trail. It's not much, I know, but there's not much fun in spending large swathes of your life unemployed either, so I celebrate joy wherever I can find it. And as this book shows, it's a joy that lasts well beyond the initial run of the play.

Made in Wales takes the process a step further though, and

introduces a luxury that few actors ever experience: the writer. The remit of the company is to develop new writing, and what could be more useful for a writer than seeing just how a play is exploded and put on its feet? Nothing can heighten a writer's awareness of craft more than experiencing first-hand exactly what is required of a piece to make it workable.

Part of the appeal of new writing lies in the fact that it doesn't follow a formula. Writers can see their work performed in front of an audience.
While I try and make a few decent acting choices.

On a slightly different tack, it's a reassuring feeling knowing that if you can't see the wood for the trees you can turn and ask the author what he meant. After you've cleared it with the director, obviously...

A new writing company has a responsibility to serve the piece, as well as serve the writer. There will always be a tension between the author and the director: each believes that they possess the ultimate vision of what the piece should be. And to a certain extent, both of these claims are valid. In purely practical terms the play is a direct result of the author's creative vision, while the director's interpretation and helmsmanship ensures that the piece reaches the audience with technical proficiency and a sense of cohesion.

That is why a director who is distanced from the text is vital. With a process that is as collaborative as creating theatre, there is no room for being precious. Compromises are necessary and decisive leadership cannot be affected by any considerations other than getting the job done. Authors, actors, designers, musical directors, choreographers, fight arrangers and lighting designers each has a part to play in the realization of a text, and it is the vision of the director that (hopefully) creates a powerful whole that is greater than the sum of its diverse parts.

This policy of inclusion by the company isn't a form of laziness, far from it. The ensuing debates often need to be curbed by a firm hand because there's only a finite amount of time in a rehearsal period. It's a conscious decision made with the express intention of fostering writing that's inherently for the theatre.

Writers are becoming more informed by the recorded media. The 'jump-cut' grammar of film and television is becoming all-pervasive, and in the present context of small casts and under-funded venues, anything more than a five-hander is a headache. So, revolving stages may solve problems for the National, but for the rest of us we need writers who understand the requirements of practical staging at the very least.

This is where Made in Wales's policy of writer inclusion begins to make sense. We need writers who write for the theatre, not people who submit rejected telly scripts. We need actors who enjoy the specific challenge of going where no performer has gone before, and we need to keep developing an audience.

Made in Wales has given me the opportunity to work and tell some pretty good stories.

I believe Made in Wales is doing, and will keep doing, all of these things because new writing is, obviously, Welsh theatre's only hope. I don't think anyone would want to have to justify regurgitating classics and nothing but classics to the public ad infinitum.

And so to :

The pieces in this book.

Safar was the first play we rehearsed for a rep. season MIW undertook at The Point in the summer of 1996. It was the first job I'd had since leaving college two days previously, although I'd worked as an actor for a few years before starting at the Welsh College of Music and Drama.

Let me make it clear from the start, Mr. Teare was scary. He kept talking about "The Turns" and "The contract with the audience." Me, I was clueless. It took me a few days - uh, weeks - to realize that he had an adversarial sense of humour. Thankfully I like being teased, it makes me laugh. And hey, paranoia is healthy in actors - it makes sure they earn their money.

The text of *Safar* was elusive, but the piece worked in front of the audiences that it drew with a palpable resonance. The laughter and the silences were steeped in recognition, it was a valuable reminder that art can do so much more than simply pass time. And because the original text was almost a poem, at points the rehearsals became like a devising project, creating solutions instead of merely uncovering them.

And so to *Gulp*. I became involved a few weeks after the end of the first run when Rebecca Gould was preparing to re-direct the show for a short tour. Due to *Gulp's* stellar performance at the box office, Chapter invited the Company to return for another successful run. We had one more date in South Wales - Newport, and then the Company left lock, stock and barrel for the far-flung shores of Free Ireland.

Roger Williams writes everyday truth alongside beautifully crafted pathos.

Susie in Gulp was a gift. She is a well rounded real person, who can shift from full-on performing fag-hag:

'I'm not talking love here Rob. I'm talking y'know, bedroom, underpants, ky jelly, orgasm. And you can't tell me that you don't want an orgasm.'

To a lonely, loveless woman desperately waiting and wanting:
'Love... proper, make-your heart go boom love.'

Gulp was an extremely successful and accessible piece that spoke of difficult matters with a human voice. Everyone from blue-haired old ladies to butch few-haired builders (you know who you are) could understand the people in the play, and by extension their predicaments. Not ignoring the cult audience that the piece garnered, it was a great example of the power of using an accessible vehicle to say something important rather than a bald polemic.

I think the revised text we used for the tour was a direct result of Roger's inclusion in the process. After listening to the show for the length of the run, I suspect he had a very specific wish-list, and the re-mounting of the show gave us all an opportunity to see the piece take a few more steps along its (on-going) evolutionary path.

My Piece of Happiness is the most recent work I've done for the company, and also the piece with which I've enjoyed the longest association. Way back during the *Safar* season, Lewis Davies brought along the beginnings of a play. It was character driven and heart-felt, and I knew I wanted to play Sean from the first morning.

Lewis writes with a minimalist voice. His characters

communicate through a disjointed and much harder speech. This textural hardness was only part of the difficulty that I experienced during rehearsals.

In the rehearsal room we quickly discovered that the text had a bizarre quality of being playable in an infinite number of ways. Not just the odd line, mind you. Every single one was an enigma, and I've no idea how he did it. This enigmatic quality turned out to be the strength of the piece. By the time the debate-charged rehearsal process had finished everyone knew everything there was to know about the world of the play.

In between the written/spoken truth lies the unwritten/ unspoken, subtextural, 'Truer' truth. In My Piece of Happiness Lewis has crafted an in-between truth.

Certain scenes ran along these two separate scripts following the rules of Text and Subtext, while certain scenes didn't. This reminded me how brave the piece was and also how much of an acting challenge. The scenes involving the central character of Sean and Sarah (my character) were according to Jeff free of any subtext. I fought this direction, pushing hard to illustrate each word Sarah spoke with at least three different colours. I was uneasy with the beautiful simplicity in the writing.

My Piece of Happiness is a love story about two adults with learning disabilities told against the back-drop of an over-stretched welfare state. For a piece of new writing that may not look too accessible at first glance, the box office was fantastic. The average house was 75% full, and that's pretty fine in anyone's book. It's also a testament to Made In Wales's growing audience at Chapter.

So there you have it.

On a much more selfish note, I hope I'll get the chance to experience the freedom and terror of the unknown a few more times yet.

And yes, that's a hint.

James Westaway
Lowri Mae
May 1998

In rehearsal   *photo: L.D.*

Heard in rehearsal

'A multiplicity of meaning or totally devoid of content.'

'The trouble with Lewis's writing, is that the acting's between the lines.'

'It's in the novel.'

Made in Wales is the main new-writing company for Welsh Theatre (in the English language). It was founded in 1982 since when it has produced approximately fifty world-premieres in Wales, England, Scotland and Ireland. In addition to these some two hundred script-in-hand or rehearsed readings have been presented as well as various festivals, seminars and symposiums. An average of eighty unsolicited manuscripts are read and reported on each year and a number of specific development projects (women writers, multi-cultural writing etc.) have also been undertaken. Writers whose work has been developed by Made In Wales are currently working in theatre, radio, television and film while a number of their plays have been published.

Recent work, other than that shown in this volume, has included a site-specific production with students from the Welsh College of Music and Drama to commemorate the eightieth anniversary of the end of the First World War (including an open-air battle scene), a production of *'Queen of Hearts'* by Christine Watkins (in which a Princess Diana look-a-like meets an obsessed transvestite) and *'Dare!'* a new musical celebrating the ambition and resilience of the young people of Wales today.

MADE IN WALES can be contacted worldwide on
madein.wales@virgin.net